T0300697

What Do I Do?

What Do I Do?

Every Wedding Etiquette Question Answered

MARIAH GRUMET

ROCK
POINT

Contents

section 3: the wedding

Welcome.

If this book has landed in your hands, it is safe to say that congratulations are certainly in order! My name is Mariah Grumet, and I am a Certified Etiquette Trainer and the founder of Old Soul Etiquette. My combined passion for etiquette and helping others to become the best version of themselves is what led me to take a huge leap of faith and leave my job in the fashion industry to create my brand, Old Soul Etiquette, in 2021.

My method of teaching puts a modern and approachable twist on timeless lessons of etiquette, manners, and respect to help my clients and community distinguish themselves, create stronger connections, and reach their full potential in their personal and professional lives.

My sole mission is to bring back an intentional sparkle to a lost art, by which I mean taking the fundamentals of what etiquette is truly about and applying it to what actually makes sense in our modern everyday lives.

I can assure you this is not your traditional or outdated wedding etiquette book. I want you to read the pages in here and feel like you are consulting a close friend and confidant. What comes to mind when you think of the word *etiquette*? I urge you to put aside any preconceived notions that etiquette is outdated, not necessary in our modern world, and only relevant to a certain group of people, or that it is considered a symbol of status and nobility.

Etiquette is for everyone, regardless of who you are, where you come from, what you do, and what your preferences are. Etiquette guidelines were and are put in place to show respect, consideration, and kindness to everyone we encounter. It ensures we are doing the right thing. Sure, many specific etiquette guidelines from past times do not apply anymore; however, etiquette evolves as we do and as our world and society does. Weddings are no exception to this.

I begin all of my courses and events with an explanation of an analogy, so it only makes sense to start this book the same way. The analogy I use is of a tool belt; I want you to imagine you are wearing a tool belt at all times. Your belt is filled with tools that consist of your unique attributes, special skills, and, ultimately, everything that makes up who you are. When you learn about modern etiquette you are simply sharpening your existing tools and/or adding new tools to your tool belt.

A full tool belt gives you a sense of preparedness, and that preparedness automatically leads to living your life with more ease and confidence. A full tool belt empowers us to approach any situation in the very best way, as the very best version of ourselves, no matter where we are, what we are doing, or who we are with. This book is filled with wedding-specific tools for you to add to your tool belt so you feel confident and prepared throughout your entire wedding experience.

I will take you through each phase and step of your planning process, starting at the very beginning and going all the way to the days following your wedding. We will tackle the potential sticky situations and stressors that may arise so you can rest assured you are handling them with poise and grace. We are going to make sure you cross your Ts and dot your Is without jeopardizing your vision, and, more importantly, your peace. We will work to balance the need of your family, guests, and vendors without forgetting about those of you and your partner. This is your complete guide to planning your wedding in a way that shows you how to do the "right" thing without compromising the day of your dreams—or your boundaries. We will discuss traditions old and new, and how to include your and your partner's personalities in your wedding plans.

My goal in writing this book is to take into consideration the many different wedding styles, family dynamics, religions, cultures, and personal preferences that each couple may have in order to create an inviting and inclusive environment. There are deep-rooted traditions when it comes to weddings, and I will walk you through these, suggesting which traditions may be important to consider keeping, which you can do away with, and how you can pour your own flavor into some.

We will also focus on the "why" behind the traditions and how you can modernize the "how," so that everything fits well with your unique wedding style. While some of the traditions may not apply to your celebration at all, my hope is this book serves as a helping hand as you plan your most magical day.

This is your go-to modern guide to all things wedding etiquette, so you can focus on what really matters: planning and executing the wedding of your dreams. Here you will find the answers to your wedding-related questions, concerns, and tricky situations that end in *"What do I do?"*

You can easily flip to a section when you need a question answered or before you embark on a certain aspect of planning. A hearty congratulations to you, and happy wedding planning!

Mariah Grumet

Pre-planning

This is a moment you've probably replayed in your head close to a million times—being asked the magic question that future married couples everywhere dream of hearing. Yes, I am talking about the sweet bliss of an engagement to your one true love. While the days immediately following your engagement ask nothing of you but to bask in bliss, it will soon be time to get to work! Planning a wedding could be categorized as a full-time job. Let's face it, trying to make everyone happy in the process is the real challenge.

In this section, we will navigate the less-glamorous jobs, the tricky conversations, and the traditions to ensure the entire wedding process is a home run from an etiquette perspective. Remember, this is all about showing your guests, vendors, and family respect and consideration while simultaneously remembering this is your day. We will cover all of the aspects of your pre-planning process, from your engagement to crunching the numbers, deciding on a venue, and coming up with your guest list among much more. This section will help set you up for success before you dive into specific details.

Your Engagement

While the majority of this book focuses on specific wedding planning etiquette, we cannot forget to start at the very beginning, you know, that big event that happens that launches you into wedding planning mode—your engagement! While you twirl around on cloud nine, there are still a few boxes to check off from an etiquette perspective when it comes to announcing and celebrating your engagement.

It seems like each weekend, without fail, everyone's social media feeds are filled with engagement announcements, baby gender-reveal videos, wedding photos, etc. Before social media existed there were newspaper announcements or formal announcements that were mailed to family and friends when a big life event took place. Our digital age causes a knee-jerk reaction for us to post our exciting news for the world to see. While you absolutely should do just that if you want to, let's hit the brakes for a moment. Have you called your fiancé's grandma first? Did you take a moment to FaceTime your aunt and young cousins who have been sitting on the edge of their seats? This will not be a book about pleasing everyone—trust me, that would simply be an impossible feat. However, your closest friends and family deserve to hear your exciting life news from you before seeing it in a social media post.

⋆» The Engagement Announcement «⋆

If you are looking to take a more formal or traditional route when it comes to announcing your engagement, consider a newspaper or mailed announcement. Engagement announcements are typically made by the bride's parents; however, there is no reason why you and your partner cannot send out your own engagement announcement, or another family member or close friend could do so on your behalf. If you would like to announce your engagement in a newspaper, be sure to contact your local paper to find out more details. For a modern approach to announcements, you can create an e-card or some type of digital message.

TIP ❥ *If you have a loved one who is elderly or unable to read for any reason, take the time to make a personal phone call as they may not be able to experience your mailed or digital announcement in the same way that the others can.*

It is perfectly acceptable to send an engagement announcement to people who may not be invited to your wedding. At this point, it's likely you and your partner have not even had the conversation about a guest list yet, so there's no need to harp over any details too much.

⁕ The Engagement Party ⁕

You've announced your engagement, and now you'll have to consider whether or not you and your partner will be having an engagement party. Engagement parties were/are traditionally hosted by the bride's parents, but today it is appropriate for any family member, friend, or even you and your partner to host your engagement celebration.

Some couples choose to celebrate immediately following the proposal, while others will choose to have a separate party or small gathering scheduled for the near future. Your engagement party can be anything from a formal dinner party to a Sunday afternoon backyard gathering, or anything in between. Because this is the very first of many celebrations to come, you will want to be mindful of your budget and reserve some money specifically for your engagement celebrations.

TIP ❯ *Engagement party invitations should be reserved for close family and friends who will also be receiving an invitation to your wedding. You do not need to invite everyone who will be invited to your wedding to the engagement party, but everyone that you ask to your engagement party also needs to be on your wedding guest list.*

While engagement parties are popular wedding events, it is one of those traditions that you can do away with depending on your personal situation or preference. If you and your partner prefer not to have one or can't have one, then it is completely okay to skip this event in the wedding process. You can find other ways to celebrate your engagement with your loved ones outside of having a party, such as a small dinner with your immediate families, finding a creative way to share your story, and/or taking and sharing engagement photos.

–» ask mariah «–
Your Engagement Questions

What is the difference between an invitation and an announcement?

An announcement is simply sharing news of a life event and does not request anyone's presence to a particular event. Gifts are not required, but some people may send them upon receiving an announcement. An invitation requires someone's presence to a particular event and gifts are standard unless stated otherwise.

TIP ❯ *Be prepared with stationery early on in the engagement process so you can thank people who choose to send you gifts upon announcing your engagement. See specific thank-you note etiquette on page 182.*

If my parents/loved ones don't approve of our relationship, should we invite them to our engagement celebrations?

Your approach to this will depend on your standing relationship with these family members and the severity of the situation. Generally speaking, it would be best to give them a personal announcement directly from you prior to sending out a formal announcement, whether by mail or digitally. While you will not have control over how they react to the news, you do have control over doing the right thing by allowing them to hear it from you first. Maybe it will go over better than you expected!

It would also be best to include them in the mailed or digital announcements, if you are going that route. I would also advise inviting them to any engagement celebrations you intend to hold, to set the tone for the rest of the planning process. This, of course, again depends on the individual situation. Unfortunately, disapproval can be communicated in a wide range of ways, and you may find yourself unable to share the exciting news based on the extremity of the situation. Consult with your partner to work together to determine the best course of action for your individual family dynamic and situation.

What if I want to go the traditional route and send a newspaper announcement but my family/loved ones live in different areas?

I would recommend opting to announce your wedding in two ways: through the newspaper, then through an additional mail or e-card. You could also acquire extra copies of the newspapers with your announcement in it to share with out-of-state family or close friends at a later time.

If it is my second or third wedding, is it still proper etiquette to do a formal announcement?

Absolutely. You have every right to celebrate this engagement in the best way that works for you! Depending on the phase of life that you are in, you may also have different friends, coworkers, etc., than you did at the time of a previous wedding.

My partner and I are different ethnicities, and our families speak different languages; what would be the best way to announce our engagement to our families?

If you are planning on mailing out announcements, consider a two-sided announcement, one for each language. If you are doing a newspaper announcement, you can ask the newspaper to include a translation to your announcement.

Should I expect to receive gifts at my engagement party?

Unless you have stated otherwise on your invitation, you can definitely expect to receive gifts from people coming to celebrate your engagement. You may even find that some guests send a gift immediately upon receiving the engagement party invitation. If someone attends your engagement party without a gift, it may be due to what their budget allows, and they are taking into consideration your other events that are coming up.

Budget

It is nearly impossible to fill in any other detail without starting at the very beginning—the budget. While money is certainly not the most comfortable topic to talk about, it is the factor that allows the rest of the planning to fall into place. You will want to prepare to think about budgeting from the start of the engagement celebrations all the way to sending thank-you notes after the wedding.

Historically, the bride's parents would pay for the entire wedding, and the groom's family would cover the costs of the rehearsal dinner and potentially the honeymoon. This is one of those traditions that can certainly still apply to some couples, but for many others, it simply does not work.

Perhaps you and your fiancé are paying for the entire wedding or perhaps you are receiving a financial contribution from both families in some way. In this day and age, individual family situations trump tradition when it comes to discussing money.

❧ Budgeting for Your Big Day ❧

How should you approach budgeting for the big day? For starters, schedule an intentional time to discuss the budget and related details together as a couple. Before you can book a venue or schedule vendors, you need to know what you're working with. Do some research together to find out approximately how much your desired venues cost or what the going rate is for various vendors in your area. You may also want to put out some feelers to see if your dream venues are even available for your preferred dates, as timing will directly affect budgeting. While it will most likely be too early to have any exact answers or plans, this will give you a good starting place to determine how much you have saved up already, how much you will want/need to continue to save, or how much your family/loved ones would need to contribute to have your desired wedding.

For couples paying for their own wedding in its entirety, time might just end up being your best friend. Deciding to wait to have your wedding gives you an opportunity to save and add to what you already have in order to create a budget that you are comfortable with. Consider setting up a separate bank account to ensure the wedding funds are not being used for any other purpose while you save and plan.

If you already know you and your partner will be paying for the wedding in its entirety, regardless of the situation, this next "talking shop with relatives" section may not apply to you. Wedding planning can potentially be a very sensitive time for certain family dynamics; you may find yourself in a situation where you do not want to talk about the financial planning process with your family at all, as it may be too delicate, or your relationship with them may not warrant a conversation like that whatsoever. It might be that your family is not in a position to assist you with your budget, but you still will want them involved in the planning process and won't want to insult them. In the end, you have to do what works for you and your partner's family dynamics.

I wasn't joking when I said money is not the most comfortable topic to talk about. If you choose to approach your loved ones about financial support, this could potentially be one of the most challenging discussions you have throughout the wedding planning process. It could also be a conversation that you stress over that ends up going smoother than you expected!

❧ Budgeting Game Plan ❧

The first chat you must have is with your fiancé to establish a game plan. *Is it polite to approach my/my partner's parents or extended family for money for our wedding? What does this conversation look like?* Unless you have previously discussed that your family or your partner's family is unable to contribute to your wedding budget, it can be appropriate to approach them with the question as long as it's asked correctly, sensitively, and tastefully.

Let's look at a very simple recipe that will help you with the money talk.

❧ A SOLID GAME PLAN ❧

You will find more success if you do some intentional planning before asking the question. You and your partner are a team in this, and you have to come up with, and perhaps even practice, the play you are going to run. Although most of your other wedding details will directly depend on the budget you come up with, it will be beneficial to you both to have a general idea of what kind of wedding you would like to have. You want to show your family that you have done your due diligence prior to approaching them with this question.

You also want to be able to give your family members a realistic figure that coincides with the type of wedding you are interested in having. This could mean researching the average cost of the style of wedding you want to have, the number of people you are picturing, etc. A backyard wedding will warrant a very different budget than a Saturday evening black-tie affair at a rented mansion. Another variable is how soon you are planning to get married.

A wedding in six months' time will obviously give you as the couple less time to save, which may mean needing to ask for more help, as opposed to having a wedding in two years' time.

You might also want to discuss your approach as a part of your game plan to ensure your team (you and your partner!) remain on the same page. The more unified you are in this plan, the easier it will be to politely deal with any pushback (which will most likely find its way to the family dinner table). Will you be asking your family for a round number? Will you tell them how much you have set aside for the wedding and let them come up with an amount from there?

Perhaps you are asking a family member to contribute to something specific, such as the cost of the DJ or the cake. Maybe you are planning on asking if they are able to contribute at all. There is not a one-size-fits-all formula for how to approach the conversation; it will depend on your family dynamic, previous conversations, or expectations you have set as a family, as well as individual financial positions. This part of the recipe is all about pitching your plan, running your play, and, ultimately, setting up yourself and your partner for success.

✤ REALISTIC EXPECTATIONS ✤

Speaking of success, this may mean you don't get the answer or number you were hoping for, or maybe even expected. It may mean a drama-free conversation that resulted in a compromise. Do not set yourself up for disappointment by having high expectations for how the conversation will pan out. Go in with an open mind and respect for both of your families' financial situations. Although this is a subject that could easily lead to frustration, you will get more bees with honey.

✦ STRAIGHTFORWARD QUESTIONS ✦

Any question that is asked with a direct sense of confidence is guaranteed to capture the audience. This is not the time to beat around the bush. What we say is important, but how we say what we say is even more crucial. It's all about your delivery; approach your question with a tone that says you've done your pre-planning, that you are asking with assurance, but you are also being considerate of what you are asking.

This is also the moment to practice your solid body language while you ask the questions. This means shoulders back, chin in line with the ground, and try to avoid fidgeting as much as you can, no matter how uncomfortable or nervous you might actually be. I urge you to be mindful of the timing of posing your question and making sure it is appropriate. Additionally, ensure the only people around when you ask are those you want involved in this conversation.

You can use the below example as a guide if you're not sure whether or not a family member(s) or loved one (s) is able to contribute:

> *"As we begin planning our wedding, we wanted to ask if you would be able or willing to contribute financially to our budget in any way. We understand this is a big ask and would welcome and love your help with the planning in any form you are able to make work."*

This approach asks the question clearly but also ends on a positive note. Ending the "big ask" this way will help diffuse any awkwardness and also offer an alternative road for the conversation to go down that will still make your loved ones feel involved despite what their financial situation may allow. It is a direct way to ask the question while still maintaining a sensitive tone, which is important.

Use the below example if you already know a family member(s) or loved one(s) plans to contribute:

"We are so grateful you have offered to financially help us plan our wedding. As we're starting to make some decisions, we want to ask how much you are willing and able to give so we can plan accordingly."

Use the below example if you would like to ask a family member for a nonmonetary contribution, especially if you will be doing many of the planning aspects on your own as a couple:

"We are so grateful that you have offered to help us with our wedding planning. We were hoping you would be able to help us with X (enter here what you need—an example of this can be baking and decorating the cupcakes for the wedding reception, helping with DIY decor, or anything else you may need)."

✦ ACCEPTANCE ✦

Make sure you are prepared to accept an answer that you may not have expected. This is not a time to argue or beg for an explanation, despite the outcome. There is a long road of planning ahead, and you do not want to ruffle feathers this early on.

✦ FLEXIBILITY ✦

Be willing to bend if a compromise is required. Remember, you don't have to bend too much; it is your day, after all.

✢ BALANCE OF POWER OVER DECISIONS ✢

If your families agree to contribute to your budget in some way you'll have to consider the balance of power over making decisions throughout the planning process. For instance, your aunt offers to purchase your wedding outfit, so does she get a say in the final choice? Let's say your aunt is insistent that you wear traditional attire that represents your culture. However, you want to wear something less traditional. Ultimately, you and your partner should wear what makes you feel your very best on your most special day. Validating your loved one and acknowledging their opinion while also placing a boundary to get what you want may be the best approach. Here is an example of what you can say in a situation like this:

> *"X (enter name here), you know how truly important your opinion is to me, and I am forever grateful you have offered to buy my wedding day attire. I know you'd want me to feel my best, but this other attire is truly my favorite."*

In this example, you are making sure that your loved one feels validated and acknowledged while also making sure you put up a boundary to get your favorite outfit for your wedding day. If your loved one is not receptive to this, you may have to find a place to compromise. Is there a traditional piece of jewelry or different accessory you can wear to accompany your less-traditional outfit of choice?

If you are receiving monetary assistance from a family member, honoring their opinions or requests (within reason) is a simple way to say "thank you." Sometimes communication and validation are all they need. I will continue to talk about the importance of your tone and delivery throughout this entire planning process. The balance of power requires compromise and respect, but ultimately it is your day. Sounds like quite the juggling act, doesn't it?

⊱ Your Nonnegotiables List ⊰

Once you have determined whether you will be receiving any financial help, or you and your partner will be responsible for paying for the entirety of the wedding, it's time to talk real numbers. There are quite a few essential factors that play a role in determining the actual budget. The first thing to do is come up with the number you have to spend. Next, make your list of nonnegotiables. This will help with big decisions. For example, if having a band is a nonnegotiable, you may have to cut back somewhere else in order to accommodate the cost.

Once you have agreed on your nonnegotiables, it's time to make your category list, which might look something like this:

- Venue (with all fees and taxes included)
- Wedding planner
- Officiant fee
- Photos and video
- Florals
- Cake
- Decor
- Music
- Invitations
- Transportation
- Travel and accommodations for you and your partner

- Rings
- Attire for you and your partner
- Shower
- Bachelorette party
- Rehearsal dinner
- Other events (bridal luncheon, welcome party, etc.)
- Gifts for your wedding party
- Tips for vendors (see the chapter on vendors)
- Any special accommodations for you, your partner, and/or guests

Each category list will differ as wedding styles differ. Your individual list will depend on things such as whether or not your venue provides food, if you have to use an outside vendor for it, or if you will be making your own. You may have a separate category for the rehearsal dinner, or perhaps you put flowers for the rehearsal, ceremony, and reception all in one category. This list is just a guide to help you get started.

At this point, you should have your budget number—whether through your anticipated savings plan, a number from loved ones, or a combination of both. You also have your list of nonnegotiables and your categories. Although you should have done some high-level research prior to this step, now would be a good time to do some more in-depth and specific research to learn the approximate realistic costs for your categories in the geographical location where your wedding is taking place. All of this pre-planning is setting you up with a strong foundation as you begin to make some big decisions.

TIP ❯ *Don't forget to leave a number for miscellaneous costs that will arise. Giving yourself a strong place to start will set you up for success throughout the wedding planning process.*

Budgeting for your wedding is no easy task, whether that's approaching family members for help, agreeing on your nonnegotiables with your partner, or plugging in all the numbers. However, setting the organizational tone for your wedding planning process from the very beginning with budgeting will prove to be very helpful as you continue. Remember, we are laying a strong foundation so you can begin to plan your wedding with more ease.

—» *ask mariah* «—
Your Budget Questions

My partner and I are having trouble seeing eye to eye on our nonnegotiables. How do we handle this so that we are both happy?

It's all about a compromise! Take the time to listen to each other to learn why your partner might consider an aspect of the wedding as nonnegotiable. Perhaps there is another area in the budget that you can agree is a place to cut back, so you can both be pleased with adding in your individual nonnegotiables. Plus, there is no limit as to how many nonnegotiables you can have. It's more about being able to determine how much of your budget remains after you've accounted for the things you are not willing to bend on.

My partner and I are having a destination wedding; how do we go about deciding our nonnegotiables and budgeting for them?

You will go about it the same way as you would if you were planning a wedding in your local area, but there will be additional things to consider. For starters, you will need to bear in mind the exchange rate and cost of goods and services in the location in which you are choosing to get married. If there is a drastic difference from what you are used to locally, you may be using up quite a lot of your budget in places you were not expecting to.

Additionally, you (and your guests!) will have the added travel and accommodation expenses. While you want your guests to be happy, comfortable, and feel at home at any wedding, you might need to take your guests' situations into consideration a bit more. Your nonnegotiables may have to do with your guests more so for a destination wedding than for a local wedding.

For example, you want to ensure the location you are booking has safe accommodation for everyone to stay in. You also may need transportation to and from the wedding site to be nonnegotiable depending on your destination, because it's more than likely that your guests will not have their own method of transportation if they have to travel by plane.

You may find yourself booking your wedding at an all-inclusive resort, and chances are they have a wedding package that includes most (if not all) of your nonnegotiables. While the process of choosing your nonnegotiables will look very similar no matter what style of wedding you are planning to have, the actual categories will differ based on the different things you have to account for in your individual wedding style.

My and my partner's parents all want to contribute to our wedding; how do we decide what each of our parents can contribute toward without offending either side?

In a traditional wedding, it would be common to see the groom's family pay for the rehearsal dinner and the bride's family pay for the wedding ceremony and reception. In modern times, if both families are able to contribute, you may want to consider having them contribute to the same or similar expenses, so the responsibility is equal and fair regardless of how much they are able to give.

For instance, you may have them both contribute to the venue or maybe the band. This way, no one is offended or feels as if they are doing less than the other. If they want to pay for something specific instead of just giving you the money, perhaps choose to assign them each a vendor service so the playing field stays as level as possible. For example, one partner's family may be responsible for the photographer/videographer, and the other may be in charge of paying for the flowers. This seems fairer than having one family pay for most of the venue while the other pays for the cake.

My or my partner's loved ones are contributing to the wedding and have different ideas for the type of wedding they want to contribute to than what we are planning for or envisioning. How do we handle this?

This is where the importance of doing some planning before your initial budget conversation with family and friends comes in. Having an idea of the wedding style you and your partner are envisioning in addition to communicating that as clearly as possible will be essential. That way, there are no surprises after funds have been exchanged.

This is also where compromise and the balance of power come in. If there is an aspect of the wedding that does not go against your nonnegotiable list but you know is important to a loved one, you may want to consider adding it in. This may be a cultural or religious aspect, or perhaps something more traditional that you were not originally considering including. For example, if you were planning on having a nontraditional wedding with no dancing, but your or your partner's mother was really counting on a first dance, perhaps that is something you will consider including.

My partner and I are an interfaith couple and want to have two different ceremonies. How do we budget for both of them?

If that is a nonnegotiable aspect of the wedding for you, having an understanding of how much each ceremony will cost will allow you to see how much of your budget you have left over to spend on other things. The two ceremonies may also be a specific expense that you ask each family to assist with. Additionally, you will have to consider a guest list for each ceremony as it may not be necessary for everyone to attend both. You may have to cut back on another section of your budget in order to have the two ceremonies. Perhaps you choose to make your own table centerpieces to free up some budget for your two ceremonies.

This is my second/third wedding, and I am over the age of fifty; do I still approach friends/family for help with our wedding budget?

This will depend on your individual situation, but it is certainly less common for family and friends to assist monetarily with a second or third wedding budget, especially if they have contributed to the previous weddings. If you find yourself in a position of needing help, perhaps ask friends or family if they can contribute to something specific, such as making the cake or centerpieces.

How do we properly accommodate guests with disabilities and/or our disabilities into our wedding budget?

If you, your partner, or a guest has a unique or special need that requires specific equipment, assistance, or accommodations, you want to ensure you are factoring this into your budget as it may come with an added expense. Depending on the specific need, to ensure you and your guests are comfortably and safely enjoying the festivities, do some research to see how much you should be budgeting to fulfill this need.

This will fall under your nonnegotiable list, as it is an important priority. It is one of those aspects of the budget that you want to factor in as early as possible so you have a true and accurate picture of what parts can go toward the details that don't fall into the nonnegotiable section. We will discuss how to approach a venue to ensure it is accommodating to a disability and/or special need in the next chapter.

Venue
&
Date

Now that you know generally how much money you have to work with, you will want to move on to the "where" and "when." Similar to how your planning couldn't happen without the budget, many of your details and next steps will not be able to fall into place without first deciding on a venue.

From a logistical standpoint, you need to set a date in order to move forward with booking vendors and such, and your date may be contingent on your desired venue's availability. You may be in a position where you know exactly what type of wedding you want to have and where. You may be in a position where you have no idea and want to shop around for options. In any case, you want to be sure you have a date or even a few alternate dates decided on before booking your venue. If a particular date is super important to you and your partner, then that may mean that you must book your venue earlier than expected to secure your desired wedding date. More about this on pages 35 to 36.

❧ Things to Consider ❧

The following is a list of things to consider when deciding on your venue and picking a date for your special day.

✧ FORMALITY ✧

How formal of a wedding do you want to have? Your venue will play an immense role in the overall formality of your event. You have to consider what "style" of wedding you envision within this, too. Do you want an outdoor ceremony? Do you want a large dance floor? Perhaps you would like a backyard wedding. Determining the formality and style of wedding will help you narrow down venue choices. We will discuss formality in more detail in a later chapter (page 68).

✧ SIZE ✧

You may not have determined your guest list yet (which we will cover in more detail soon), but the size of your wedding and the venue you choose will directly impact each other. This goes back to your list of nonnegotiables and weighing up your options.

If having a big wedding with your large extended family is important to you, you will need to find a venue that can accommodate a larger guest list. However, you may also be set on a certain venue that may leave you with no other option than to limit your guest list. Locking in your dream venue will allow you to curate your guest list accordingly.

✤ LOCATION ✤

Do you want to get married somewhere close to home, or does your heart desire a destination wedding? If you are having your ceremony at a different location than the reception, this will open up the discussion of your guests' travel requirements. These are important questions to ask yourself as you decide on a general geographical location. It is imperative to take the time to not only visit exact venues before making any decisions, but also to get a feel for the surrounding area and general location of your top venues.

✤ AVAILABILITY AND DATE ✤

The venue should be the first thing on your planning list that you secure because of how far in advance you need to do so. When choosing a venue, you may have to be flexible with the exact date you had in mind. Your date could very well be a very simple decision as it may be determined or limited by your venue's availability.

When contemplating the exact date or even the time of year/season in which to have your wedding, you'll want to consider a few things. Is there a specific season in which you and your partner picture getting married? Are there any special dates that it may overlap with, such as family birthdays, anniversaries, holidays, etc.? While there is no specific rule against planning your wedding date on certain birthdays, anniversaries, holidays, etc. it may affect how many people show up to your wedding as people may have plans or uphold certain traditions during these times. You also don't want to offend anyone if planning on a specific holiday. However, if you decide to have your wedding date on a specific holiday, such as having a wedding on Christmas, keep in mind that the price of your venue and vendors may be higher. You may not be able to avoid certain birthdays or anniversaries as it may be dependent on the availability of your venue and budget.

TIP ❯ *You will want to research if there are any special events happening in the general location where you are getting married that may directly impact accommodation, transportation, and even budgeting. For instance, if the city you are getting married in is having its big marathon race on the same weekend as your wedding, hotels may be limited and more expensive, and the crowds may be overwhelming and distracting.*

The last thing you'll want to consider when it comes to a date is how long of an engagement you want to have. Again, you may be at the mercy of your venue's availability. Depending on your desired wedding style, you may need at least a year to plan and book vendors in advance. If your wedding is less formal or requires less planning/budgeting, you may not want a long engagement. Perhaps you are saving for your wedding budget and need to plan for a long engagement. Put some true thought into the date before committing to it, to ensure it works well for your wants and needs.

Being flexible with both your date and time of day may help you land your dream venue. There are ways for you to get creative if at first glance a venue that you have your eye on seems out of budget. You may find that some venues offer lower rates for weekday weddings versus weekend weddings or offer lower rates for a daytime wedding versus an evening wedding. These will be factors that you and your significant other will have to consider when choosing a specific date. If you're deciding on a weekday wedding, keep in mind that your expected attending guest list may change from that of a weekend wedding due to everyone's personal schedules.

✦ PRICE ✦

Will your budget support this venue? This is one of the most important questions to ask yourself during the venue shopping process. Does the venue offer different packages, rooms, services, or wedding styles so you can work within your budget?

✦ CULTURAL/RELIGIOUS TRADITIONS ✦

When determining the best venue for your dream wedding, you want to consider whether or not a location has the capacity for you to carry out any specific traditions that incorporate both your and your partner's religion and culture.

✦ VENUE ACCESSIBILITY ✦

When visiting venues, you will want to consider accessibility depending on your guest list and their unique needs. This may mean accessible parking, restrooms, entrances, or any special services that they provide.

There are many different factors to consider when you are shopping around for the right venue. Remember, the earlier the better when it comes to selecting a venue so you can ensure you are booking the venue of your dreams, and so there is plenty of time to start working on the rest of the planning.

—» ask mariah «—
Your Venue & Date Questions

When choosing a venue, how can I accommodate guests with disabilities/our disabilities?

The best way to handle this is to have it be one of the main questions you ask the venue when touring different options. You can ask them if they are able to accommodate the specific need, and if not, what measures you can take or what an additional cost may be in order to have this need accommodated.

Depending on what you or your guest requires to be comfortable and safe, you may have to contact a vendor to see how things would work with the specific venue. Most venues will be very willing and able to help accommodate you and your guests, but you have to ensure you are up front with your questions and expectations to ensure you are getting the result you want and need.

I am having a destination wedding. What is the etiquette around destination weddings so I can ensure my guests feel comfortable attending?

A destination wedding may result in a smaller guest count as the expense will be greater for your attendees. Not everyone will have the means to attend. Don't take this personally. For starters, you will want to notify your guests of the date and location of the wedding at an earlier time than you would for a local wedding. (See the invitations and save-the-dates chapters.) As the couple who is getting married, you are not responsible for covering the travel or accommodation for your guests.

For this reason, you will have to consider the cost of both of those pieces as they will fall on your guests. Because of the higher expense, your guests may not be in a position to spend additional money on an elaborate gift. You'd also want to ensure you are giving guests enough time to save if needed to be able to attend. Six months may not be enough time for a guest to save up traveling for your wedding as perhaps a year will.

TIP ❯ *It is polite to offer a few options for lodging if possible, so that your guests can make their decision based on their individual financial situations and preferences. With listing the accommodation options, you will also want to consider providing extra information and/or an itinerary of activities for your guests while they are staying in this location.*

How can we make sure our venue is supportive of the nontraditional style of wedding we want to have?

When you begin having the initial conversations with venues, whether over the phone or in person for a tour (or both!), communicate your vision to them up front. Painting them a picture of your personal preferences, cultural traditions, and wedding style will help them get a better idea of whether or not they are open or able to accommodate them.

It is important that the venue you choose is supportive of whatever style of wedding you are envisioning. With that, you want to prioritize asking the right questions up front to ensure your venue will be respectful of you, your partner, and your special day. Beyond this, take some time to do some further research through reviews or previous weddings to see if they've hosted weddings similar to the one you and your partner are having.

Booking Vendors

Your vendors will supply services needed for your wedding that your venue does not supply. You may not need a certain vendor if your specific venue provides the service. In some cases, vendors book as far ahead as the venues do, so you want to ensure you have a game plan to execute immediately upon securing your location and date. This means conducting your own research and perhaps asking your friends, family, or even your venue for recommendations.

Let's start at the very beginning. Will you be working with a wedding planner? This is something that you may have considered when determining your budget. If you do choose to work with a planner, they will be able to assist you in the process of finding the right vendors for your special day. While this could potentially be a huge weight off your shoulders, it certainly comes with a price tag. If you will not be using a wedding planner, it's time for you to start the vendor hunt. We will dive into a list of vendors in a bit. Check to see if your venue requires a "Day-of Planner." Some venues will require this planner or coordinator who will act as the liaison between your venue staff and the rest of your vendors. This does not have to be a planner that you work with throughout the entire process, but will be an additional vendor you have to account for and budget for.

✵ Choosing Vendors for Your Wedding ✵

When it comes to working with your vendors, whether that be your venue, your wedding planner, or anyone else involved, you want to be a gracious client. Yes, they are working for you and you are paying them to complete a job, but it is imperative to treat anyone performing a service for us with the utmost amount of respect. This is truly built from carrying out your end of the agreement. You can ensure you are successful at this by communicating your expectations up front, asking the right questions to ensure their services are in line with what you want, adhering to your vendors' policies and deadlines, and being both patient and respectful even when you need to request a change or bring up an issue.

When choosing vendors, it is in your best interest to either meet them in person or schedule a phone call or video call as well as visit their social media channels, websites, and reviews prior to signing any contract. Many of these individuals will be present for intimate parts of your day, for example, your photographer and/or videographer. You want to ensure you are not only building a professional relationship with them but that you can also be comfortable having them present for those special moments. A vendor and client relationship is just that, a relationship! Both parties must do their part and play their role to the best of their ability in order for it to be a successful relationship. Planning your wedding is going to cause some stress; it's inevitable! No amount of stress counts as an excuse to treat a vendor poorly.

When you think you've been clear enough in your communication and thorough enough in reading the small print, take it one step further. While good communication will not prevent any issues from occurring, the more you communicate up front, the less likely it will be that a serious issue will arise on the day of. As mentioned earlier, this relationship is a two-way street, so you have every right to respectfully inquire as to why your vendor has not lived up to their end of the agreement, if need be.

Here is a list of some potential main vendors. Remember, this will depend on exactly what your venue is able to provide, what you are doing yourself/with your family, and what your budget allows.

✦ FOOD/DRINK ✦

Will you need to bring in food and drinks, or is this something your venue handles? Will you need to hire a catering team and/or bartender? Will you be having a buffet or a sit-down dinner? Do you need to consider food for a cocktail hour?

✦ MUSIC ✦

Will you be outsourcing music through a DJ or a band? Or maybe you want both? Or perhaps you will be creating your own playlist and using a speaker?

✦ CAKE ✦

You can't cut the cake without one! If you are serving any additional dessert, will that be provided by your cake maker, the venue, or the caterer? If you choose not to have a cake, will you be outsourcing dessert or making your own?

✦ FLOWERS ✦

You may want to use a florist to dress up your tables and help romanticize your ceremony, but don't forget the bridal bouquet(s), groom boutonniere(s), wedding party bouquets and boutonnieres, and any additional florals for family members, if you choose to have them. You can also choose to create your own bouquets, use faux flowers, or perhaps you are not interested in having flowers at your wedding at all.

✧ DECOR/RENTALS ✧

Does your venue provide tables and chairs? How about linens and additional decor? Don't forget about those charger plates, too. You may find yourself at a venue that covers all of this, but if not, you may have to do everything à la carte.

✧ STATIONERY ✧

Your stationery designer will handle your save-the-dates and invitations, but they can also provide day-of stationery, such as menus, programs, signs, etc. We will get into the specifics of save-the-date and invitation etiquette later in the book.

✧ HAIR AND MAKEUP TEAM ✧

You will have to consider who, if anyone, is helping you get ready for your special day. Perhaps you will have a team for your closest family members and the wedding party, too. More on this later.

✧ PHOTOGRAPHERS AND VIDEOGRAPHERS ✧

If you want to hire a professional team to capture your special day, you will need to book a photographer and/or videographer.

✧ TRANSPORTATION ✧

If you are planning on taking transportation as a couple or for your immediate family, you will need to arrange this in advance. Additionally, you want to consider whether you are offering transportation for your guests such as a bus ride to and from the ceremony and/or reception—this is especially important if you are having a destination wedding.

TIP ➤ *Even though a ceremony officiant is not technically a vendor, it is important to have them in mind when planning your wedding, because you will have to make sure they are available for your wedding date.*

Each vendor, depending on their area of specialty, will differ in how hands-on they are on the day of your wedding or other events. For instance, your stationery vendor will obviously not be active on the day of your wedding, whereas your DJ will be. Two things you want to keep in mind for "day-of" vendors is feeding them and tipping them. Let's begin with tipping. A "day-of" vendor would be any vendor who is performing the service the day of the wedding, such as the person setting up for your flowers or bartenders. Vendors who own their own businesses do not need to be tipped, but do not forget about their assistants. Another exception to this is if a service charge has already been indicated in a contract or bill. Don't forget to read everything through, then one extra time for good measure!

TIP ❯ *A customary tip in the U.S. is between 15 to 20 percent. You can tip your vendors upon completion of their service. If you are not present for this, a hand-written thank-you note with gratuity included is the perfect alternative.*

This list includes vendors in which the etiquette is that it is expected to tip them. You can, of course, tip other vendors for exceptional service if you would like to.

- Hair stylist
- Makeup artist
- Floral/decor setup staff
- Musicians/DJ
- Reception venue staff
- Transportation company staff
- Photographer
- Videographer

You also want to plan to feed the vendors that are with you throughout the day or evening. This could be your wedding planner and their assistants, your photography and videography team, your band or DJ, etc. You do not need to feed vendors who are simply dropping something off or setting something up. Make sure you communicate with your venue as to exactly how many vendors will be eating, so they can plan the amount of food and a location for them accordingly. Vendors can be a massive help in executing the wedding of your dreams where your budget allows. Clear and considerate communication up front and throughout the process will help make the experience as seamless as possible.

—» ask mariah «—
Your Vendor Questions

How do I handle a challenging vendor that continues to push back on my questions and requests?

Despite your organized approach, clear expectations, and respectful communication, it may still be a bumpy road with a particular vendor. Perhaps the vendor is not as responsive as you hoped they would be, or they could potentially be late in delivering you something on your agreed timeline. If you find yourself in this situation, my number one piece of advice is to pick up the phone! Much of your communication with vendors will be executed through email, but if you need to get a hold of someone and want your message to get across, give them a call. You will find that you can accomplish so much more than you would have if you continued to resort to email.

What do I do if our vendor cancels on us?

Don't panic! First and foremost, ensure there is a cancellation policy or contingency plan set in place within the contract should an unexpected circumstance arise (make sure you check this before signing a contract with a vendor). If they do cancel and it is well in advance, work with them to find out if any of their contacts and connections might be able to take over the job, or partner with your venue to see if they have a list of recommended vendors. You might also consider keeping the list of vendors that you started with when you began researching, in the event that you have to revisit this list.

What do we do if we want to have a local wedding but there is no local makeup artist or hairstylist that fits our needs?

You have two options here: you can consider doing your own hair and makeup or lean on a friend or family member for help, or you can make the investment to have an out-of-town stylist travel to you, if that is within your budget and/or is something that is important to you.

How can we make sure our vendors are the right fit for the nontraditional style of wedding we want to have?

The same thing applies to your vendors as it does to making sure your venue can accommodate your unique requests! Inquire about past weddings they have been involved in that may be less traditional for any reason. Utilize their social media photographs and reviews to learn more about their capabilities. Communicating your vision early on will help you determine which vendors best fit your needs.

How should we go about booking vendors for our destination wedding?

Bringing local vendors to your destination wedding would come with quite the price tag. It is likely that the best option for you and your partner (and your budget!) would be to source vendors that are local to your destination. Many venues will have a list of their preferred vendors. Don't be afraid to lean on them for assistance. That said, you can always do your own research, too. Be mindful of a potential language barrier when having to ask your questions and discuss details with these vendors.

If you choose to use a wedding planner, you will find that some specialize in destination weddings in specific locations. They may live and work where you live, but they factor in planning and traveling with you to your destination wedding in their pricing. If this fits in your budget, it may be helpful as they most likely have relationships with other vendors and will help make the process seamless. If you are having your wedding in an all-inclusive resort, then you may find that a wedding planner is already included in your wedding package, and you might want to ask them for assistance in finding/locating local vendors to that area.

Guest
List

Your time-sensitive things are booked, so now it's time to move down your pre-planning checklist. Next up: the guest list. Putting together your guest list is no easy feat. You will first, of course, have to determine the number of guests that your venue and budget allow for. It continues to be a theme throughout this book, but start with your nonnegotiables.

Create your list of immediate family, wedding party, closest friends, and all of their partners/spouses. This will act as your foundation, and you can build from there. Type these names into a list and categorize them into colors, starting with the nonnegotiables. Then move on to other categories—these will look different for each couple; perhaps your categories are red for extended family, blue for school friends, and green for work friends, plus-ones, parents' friends, etc. Finally, have a serious conversation with your fiancé to determine the "hierarchy" of your categories. I will explain more about this in a bit!

✥ Inviting Children to Your Wedding ✥

Another point that you will have to both decide on and be consistent with is whether or not you will be inviting children to your wedding—regardless of whether your own children will be attending. You must consider how much extra space there is on your guest list, and if your venue/style of wedding is appropriate to host children. It is absolutely acceptable to have a child-free wedding if that is what you and your partner desire. While it may be tricky if you come from a big family or have loved ones financially contributing, once you decide what is best for your individual wedding, that will become your rule across the board. While it is ultimately up to you how you decide to structure your guest list, you do not want to invite one of your friend's children and not the other. Keep it consistent whether that be no children, only immediate family who are children, or inviting everyone's children. Of course, there will always be guests you will feel obligated to invite and this is where your list of nonnegotiables will come into play.

✥ Deciding Who to Invite ✥

You may find yourself in a situation where there are family members you feel obligated to invite, but perhaps you don't have a great relationship with them, or simply don't know them very well. Ultimately, this is one of the most important days in your life and you want to be surrounded by special people who are active in your life. You certainly do not have to feel guilty about not inviting people out of obligation or duty.

Start with your nonnegotiables list of immediate family and closest friends, so you have an exact idea of how much extra space you have on your guest list. Do you remember when you were younger and you had a birthday party, and you couldn't just invite half of the class? The same goes for distant relatives, friends of your parents or grandparents, etc. It's a slippery slope when you begin to extend invitations to people you are not entirely close with. It opens the "If I invite the Smiths, I have to invite the Clarks" door. Consider brainstorming with your parents, guardians, or siblings. You can show them your guest list and ask if there is anyone they suggest you add. If someone is contributing to your budget and insists on giving someone an invitation, you can honor that to a certain extent. It is your day and your guest list, so you can compromise without settling!

HERE ARE SOME QUESTIONS TO ASK WHEN
✦ CREATING A GUEST LIST ✦

Is this person a family member?	Yes or No
Has this person met my fiancé?	Yes or No
Does this person get along with me and my fiancé?	Yes or No
Is this person supportive of our relationship?	Yes or No
Do I or my partner keep in regular contact with this person?	Yes or No
Are we inviting this person because it will make someone else happy or because someone told us to?	Yes or No
Do we want this person to show up in our wedding pictures?	Yes or No
Do we plan to keep contact with this person for years to come?	Yes or No
Will this person cause drama if they attend our wedding?	Yes or No
Is this person an ex or past crush?	Yes or No
Would I be offended if I and my partner were not invited to their wedding?	Yes or No
Does my gut tell me to invite them?	Yes or No

—» ask mariah «—
Your Guest List Questions

My wedding will be the first time my parents are in the same room together since their messy divorce. How do I diffuse this ticking time bomb?

For starters, consider having an open conversation with them both separately, assuming your relationship with them warrants this. Ask them what you can do to make them as comfortable as possible, whether that is about where they sit at the reception or ceremony, how and when they walk down the aisle, or offering separate photo times. They will appreciate you taking their needs into consideration as it's probably just as uncomfortable for them as it is for you.

In this conversation, while you acknowledge their feelings and concerns, you also want to be up front about your expectations. Tell your parents that you will do everything you can to make them feel at ease, but you would really appreciate it if they handle everything in the best possible way they can for you and your special day. What about inviting new partners or plus-ones? By not giving divorced parents a plus-one (which is different from inviting an established partner) you may be avoiding a major conflict on the day of.

Do we need to give every unmarried guest a plus-one?

The short answer is no. Determining invitations for plus-ones is directly dependent on what your budget and space allow. However, keep in mind that a plus-one and someone's serious partner are two different things. A good rule of thumb to follow is that engaged, married, serious long-term couples, and couples who live together should be invited to your wedding as a couple.

Should we expect a gift from a guest's plus-one?

Plus-ones are not responsible for bringing their own gift as they were not personally invited to the wedding by the hosts. The guest that they do accompany may give a gift from both of them. Whether or not the plus-one contributes to the gift is something decided between them and your guest.

There are members of our family who do not support our engagement. How do we navigate whether or not to invite them to the wedding?

There is not a one-size-fits-all response to this question, as it is truly situational. If there are members of your family who have been blatantly unsupportive and hurtful, you absolutely do not need to extend an invitation to them. If you aren't exactly sure, give it a try! They can always RSVP "no," but at least you did the right thing. You want to have a wedding with a room filled with people who love and support you unconditionally. Anything less than that can stay at the door!

I am on friendly terms with my ex. Do I send them an invitation to my wedding?

Well, it depends on the relationship! Are they part of your large friend group, and would it be rude to leave them out? Are they a parent to your children and it is important to you to have them there for your children? How does your partner feel about this? The most important thing is that you communicate clearly with your partner to see if they are comfortable with it. If you agree that it makes the most sense to have them there and everyone is happy with it, of course you can invite them!

Do I have to reciprocate an invitation to someone else's wedding?

You are not obligated to invite someone to your wedding simply because you were invited to theirs. Every single wedding guest list will look different for the reasons we've discussed.

What happens when our guest list has exceeded capacity and we need to "cut back"? How do we determine who stays and who goes?

There are many reasons as to why you may need to cut back on your guest list. Perhaps your dream venue has a smaller capacity than you expected, or perhaps you are looking for a more intimate experience with a smaller number of people. The most important thing here is to complete this process well before save-the-dates and/or invitations are sent out, to avoid running into a very sticky situation.

This is where your color system will come in. Remember when I told you to put your nonnegotiables in a color? Let's say you chose red for your nonnegotiable guests; you can easily visualize that each person in red needs to stay on the list. There is not a one-size-fits-all answer for who to eliminate, and it may be a lengthy process, but having your guests divided into these categories will help you visualize and prioritize what your final guest list will look like.

What about the opposite problem? Our venue notified us that we have room to invite additional people after we've already sent out save-the-dates? Should we invite more people at this point?

I recommend against inviting more people to your wedding after your save-the-dates have been sent out, unless you do it within a one-week window. Many people will create a backup list if their venue allows more people at the last minute, people respond to the save-the-date saying they are unable to attend, or even after RSVPs start coming in. The issue with this is that you don't want anyone to know they were on this "backup" list. While save-the-dates are not sent with a response request, you may have a guest notify you that they have a previous commitment on the same date as your wedding.

If someone instantly responds to your save-the-date notifying you that they are unable to make the wedding, you can quickly send out another save-the-date to someone else to fill their spot. It truly only works if you can do it quickly (within a week or so). With how active social media is in our lives, it is nearly impossible to get away with inviting someone at a later time without them knowing it was later when your other friends are posting pictures of your save-the-date on social media. Put yourself in their shoes—how would you feel if you knew you were invited after the rest of the guest list, regardless of the reasoning?

How do I handle talking about my wedding with people who I am not able to invite, such as work friends?

You may find yourself interacting with people who are not on your guest list but who want to talk about every detail of your wedding. It can certainly feel uncomfortable discussing the minutiae of your wedding, especially if this person is expecting an invitation. If you are faced with this situation, the best thing to do is lead with gratitude, as they are probably just excited for you, give a sincere yet vague response, and change the subject. Remember, you do not need to feel guilty or obligated to reveal everything or to invite anyone that you and your partner do not want to on your special day.

My or my partner's parents are significantly contributing to the wedding financially; do they get to add people to the guest list that we otherwise would not? Or they insist on inviting many more people to our wedding than my partner and I originally wanted. How do we handle this?

If this happens to you, or something similar, then you or your partner may want to approach your parents and have a conversation about the guest list. Acknowledging how much their contribution means to you while also offering a compromise may be the best option. Here is an example of what you and your partner can say to your or your partner's parents in a situation like this:

"We are so thankful for your help with this wedding. We couldn't do this without you. I want to address the added guests on our list. We really wanted to keep the number to a hundred, so perhaps we can go through your list and see who is nonnegotiable?"

—◇◇◇—

In this example, you and your partner are meeting your parents halfway by first acknowledging how much the financial help means to you but then offering a compromise. Now, issues that arise when family members pull the "Well, I'm paying for the wedding" card are almost inevitable. While you can't control how the family members will react to your compromise or suggestions, you can control how you approach the situation. Ultimately, it is your day and it's up to you and your partner to decide what is best for you.

How do I navigate the guest list for a destination wedding? Do I still invite people I know can't come but who are dear to me?

In this case, you want to consider what "can't come" really means. From an etiquette perspective, you want to send out an invitation to anyone who is on your list, without assuming what their response may be. They may have communicated prior to official save-the-dates or invitations that they will not be able to afford it or get the time off from work, but you will still want to send them a save-the-date and invitation. There is a chance their original plans or thoughts have changed by the time the save-the-dates go out, and the last thing you want to do is leave anyone out. When it comes to destination weddings, you have to expect that your final guest list may end up being smaller than your original one as some people may not be able to swing the travel plans, whether that be due to work, finances, children, etc.

How do we politely communicate to our guests that we don't want kids at our wedding?

You will be communicating that you and your partner have decided on a child-free wedding through the way in which your invitations are addressed (see the save-the-date and invitations chapters). You can also add something to your wedding website (see the website chapter). You can say something that indicates how special children are to you, but your wedding space restrictions have left you with no other option than for it to be a child-free day. This also applies even if you will be including your own children in your wedding, or certain children (e.g., if you want to have a flower girl but don't want kids at your wedding); you will still communicate your preference to your guests across the board through your wedding website and/or invitations.

If you have certain guests who do not want to respect this boundary and choose to challenge you for not wanting to have children on the day, approach your response with kindness. Explain to them that you would love to have all of the children in your life to celebrate with you, but you are restricted by your budget and space. You do not owe anyone an in-depth explanation, as this is the path you and your partner decided to take.

Wedding Party

Let's dive deeper into one of the important groups on your guest list, and that is your wedding party. Whether or not to have a wedding party is a completely personal decision between you and your partner.

The tradition of having bridesmaids stems back to ancient Rome, when they would protect the bride from any type of evil on her wedding day. As time went on, the purpose of a wedding party was and still is to assist the couple getting married by helping with events, participating in pre-wedding activities such as bach trips, and, of course, supporting the couple on their wedding day.

Today, being a part of a wedding party has evolved to be quite an expensive and elaborate role, but it certainly does not have to be. While your team of closest friends and family members accept this position as a way to support you, there are things you can do to respect their commitment and keep things reasonable and fair for all. Accepting an invitation to be a member of the wedding party comes with a significant commitment in terms of both finances and time.

⋙ Wedding Party Roles ⋘

While you will not have everything perfectly sorted out upon asking people to be part of your wedding party, you can provide a general idea of your plans and ideas. Even a simple acknowledgment that you understand how much of a commitment it is and how much you appreciate and respect them will go a very, very long way. Communicating clearly from the beginning will help avoid as much drama as possible. Your wedding party will already be spending a lot of money and time on your wedding, so you don't want to spring any surprises at the last minute.

TIP ➤ *As the person getting married, it's important for you to understand what your wedding party's responsibilities are so you can set proper expectations. Plan ahead so you can communicate these expectations up front, and the individuals you ask to be a part of your special day can make an informed decision about whether or not they are able to commit.*

Some typical bridal party expenses are, but are not limited to: a bridal shower gift, the bridesmaid's dress, shoes, accessories, the bachelorette trip—including some or all of the bride's expenses for that trip—travel, hotel accommodation for the wedding, and a wedding gift. The groomsmen can typically expect to pay for their outfit for the day of, bachelor party expenses, travel, accommodation, and a wedding gift.

A person of honor will have the most responsibility through their role in your wedding party. These are the individuals you will lean on most and communicate with most often. They will be the leaders of the rest of the wedding party, and will help plan and organize different events and things leading up to your wedding day. People of honor often take on the role of planning the bach parties, creating surprises for the couple. In a traditional wedding, when it comes to the actual day of the wedding, the maid of honor will have duties such as holding bouquets, fixing the bride's dress, helping to "put out any fires," and giving a toast or speech at the reception.

The best man's responsibilities will mirror those of the maid or matrons of honor, including a toast or speech at the reception as well. The people you choose for these positions may also incur a slightly higher cost than the rest of your wedding party; however, in modern times it is typical for the wedding party to split many of the expenses.

A wedding party is a wonderful way to involve and honor your best friends and closest family members as a part of your special day. The details for how you approach everything wedding party related will be completely up to you and your partner. The biggest takeaway I want you to leave this chapter with is how to be a gracious "host" to your wedding party by communicating finances, time commitments, and expectations up front, so that it is fun and fair for everyone involved.

✦ COMMITMENTS TO SHARE WITH YOUR WEDDING PARTY ✦

Here's a list of commitments you want to make sure you tell your wedding party up front if you decide to do any of these things so they can make an informed decision about participating in your wedding:

- Engagement party commitments
- Bach trips and any other travel expense
- Bridal and/or wedding showers
- Bridal luncheon and/or any event you want them to be a part of or help you with
- Any other miscellaneous things they would need to be in charge of or help you with (such as decorations, event setup, communicating among wedding party members, etc.)
- Outfits and shoe expectations for the day of the wedding and any other wedding-related events
- Accessories
- Specific hairstyles and/or makeup for the day of the wedding
- Any toasts or speeches that they would need to be part of
- Gifts

-» ask mariah «-
Wedding Party Questions

What is a good number of people to have in a wedding party without it being too much or seeming too small?

There is no true rule as to the number of people to have in your wedding party. A smaller number is often easier to manage, but it is entirely up to you and your partner. Another thing to note is keeping the number relatively even (it does not have to be perfect!) on both sides for logistics such as the procession and recession. On the smaller end, you may have three people on each side, and on the larger end you may have up to eight to ten people on each side.

Are there any expenses that we as the couple should cover for our wedding party if we decide to have one?

With the exception of the dress and/or tuxedo/suit, anything that you are "requiring" your wedding party to do or wear should be covered by you. For example, if you would like all of your bridesmaids to wear the same pajamas on the morning of your wedding, this is something you would want to consider purchasing and gifting to them. The same thing applies to a certain type of jewelry for the wedding day or accessories for the bachelorette trip. These items would be for them to keep, so they act as gifts for your bridal party as well. If you would like all of your bridesmaids to have their hair and makeup professionally done, this is also something that you would want to consider covering the cost for. If you are giving them the option of using a professional for their hair or makeup themselves, it's perfectly acceptable to have them pay for it, because it is not required.

Another expense that you may want to cover as an extra gesture is accommodation for the wedding weekend for the wedding party, if your budget allows. In modern days, it is more common for a couple to cover some of their expenses on their bach trips, as things have become much more expensive. Your bridal party may pitch in to cover your meals or accommodation. Lastly, if your budget allows, you may provide small gifts when asking your loved ones to be in your wedding party, at the bach trips, and on your wedding day.

How do I properly ask my friend or family member to be a part of my wedding party?

You want to give people plenty of time and notice for the role they will be playing. Asking eight months prior to your wedding is a good standard to follow. Once you've determined who will be in your wedding party, you want to honor your maid or matron of honor and/or best man by asking them first. Not only is this because they have the biggest role and you want to get their acceptance before asking the rest of the wedding party, but also because having an intimate moment to ask them first is a way to truly honor and respect the role you are asking them to play in such an important season of your life. They will be the leaders of the group, and you want to take the extra step in giving them a noteworthy moment before asking everyone else.

Once you've asked your people of honor and received their acceptance, it's truly a personal decision as to how you decide to ask the rest of your wedding party. If all or most of them live local to you, you can get them together for a special luncheon or dinner to ask. At your gathering, you might consider having small gift boxes for them to open with the question included for a personal touch. It will be much more about the gesture than what is in the actual gift box. You do not by any means need to offer a small gift in order for the question to still mean just as much. If you are not able to get everyone together in person, you could send a gift box or handwritten note to their home for a surprise or call them on the phone to ask. You are asking them to play a very important role in a monumental day in your life, so you want to ensure you display your gratitude from the very beginning by making it as special as possible.

We are an LGBTQ+ couple; how do we select our wedding party?

Your wedding party should be made up of your closest friends and family members, regardless of gender or preference. You can choose which members stand on which side during the ceremony, you can choose if you would like to have two maids or matrons of honor, or two best men, or none at all.

Feel empowered to make decisions that reflect your relationship and the wedding you dream of, not what society tells you that you should do. You can still follow all of the etiquette guidelines of respecting people's finances and everything else we've discussed in this chapter, regardless of who you decide to have or how you decide to organize your wedding party.

If this is my second or third wedding, should I have a wedding party?

You absolutely could if you wanted to. You may want to consider if you've had a wedding party in a past wedding. Would you be asking the same people? Have they already contributed financially to showers, trips, outfits, etc.? Perhaps you want to have a wedding party but it will be less of a time and money commitment this time around. If you or your partner has children, you may want to consider including them in your wedding party. It can make them feel special to be part of such an important day.

Should I expect a wedding gift from my wedding party?

Yes! Members of your wedding party should give you and your partner a gift just as any wedding guest would. However, because of the acquired expenses leading up to the wedding, they may not be in a position to give as much as a typical wedding guest. You may receive a group gift from your wedding party as this is seen sometimes. No matter how small or inexpensive, your wedding party members should be giving some sort of gift. It is much more about the gesture than it is the monetary value of the gift.

What if I don't want to have a wedding party, but still want my close friends or family members involved?

As mentioned throughout this book, there are traditions you will want to keep alive through your wedding, and there are others that will not work for you. You are allowed to make your own "rules." There are ways you can involve your closest friends or family members in different events leading up to your wedding and at your wedding without necessarily having to designate a specific wedding party, if that is not a vision you have.

TIP ❯ *If you do not want to have a wedding party, you can still invite a group of your closest friends on a trip to celebrate your wedding in place of a bach party. You can also invite some of your close friends to take photographs with you on your wedding day. Or perhaps you have your siblings stand next to you at your ceremony for the support, without the rest of the duties or activities occurring.*

No matter what you choose to do, there are still ways you can show your family and closest friends how special they are to you without compromising your vision. In the end, they will understand why you may not want a wedding party and will most likely be thankful that you found a way to still make them part of such a special day.

Do I have to include someone in my wedding party who included me in their wedding party?

The short answer is no; however, it depends on the situation. If you still have a strong relationship with this person, it may be something you consider. If a good amount of time has passed since their wedding, your relationship has changed, and you have other, closer friends now, there is nothing wrong with deciding not to have them as a member of your wedding party.

What if I asked someone to be a part of my wedding party and they committed, but then they decided to back out at the last minute?

While this is a very unfortunate scenario for so many reasons, there are not a ton of things you can do about it. To start, lead with empathy. It is likely they have a justified reason as to why they are not able to carry out their duties anymore. Once you find out the reason why they had to back out, you may consider offering for them to help out in another way, such as setting up for an event, if that makes sense for the specific situation.

I want to include both my sibling and my best friend in my wedding party. How do I choose a person of honor without offending anyone?

It is very common in modern weddings for someone to have multiple people of honor, whether that is two sisters they do not want to choose between, or a sibling and a best friend they want both involved. You may not want to exceed more than two, but you absolutely do not have to feel pressured to choose only one.

If you find yourself in this situation but feel strongly about only having one person of honor (one for you, and one for your partner), you may have to consider choosing the person you feel will be the most capable to carry out the responsibility that this position requires. You can honor the other person by asking them to help you with a specific task, or even ask them to speak at your rehearsal dinner, or other event.

I have a small family and group of friends, but my partner has a huge family and friend group and I'm not sure if I want a big a wedding party; how do we handle this?

Make sure that you communicate this early on as one of your nonnegotiables or something that is really important to you. The same thing applies when there is someone your partner insists on having in the wedding party, but you do not get along with them very well. Your partner may have to make some difficult decisions and compromises, so communicating this as early as possible will help give them plenty of time to do so.

In modern weddings, many people will have a smaller wedding party, but invite a larger group for a nontraditional bach party. For example, your partner may choose to only put family members in the wedding party, but also invite friends for a large bach celebration.

What should I consider when choosing a wedding party?

Begin with making a list of your closest friends and immediate family that you would want to involve in such a big part of this entire process, from the planning process to the events in between to the actual wedding day. Consider your relationship with each person first and foremost, keeping in mind how supportive they are of you and your partner.

Next, mull over whether or not you think they will be the right person for this level of responsibility. How much do you trust them? Do you truly want them standing by your side for this extremely important chapter of your life, or do you feel obligated to add them in? There are many things to consider when coming up with your wedding party, including who is contributing financially, but it is ultimately a decision entirely up to you and your partner.

Formality
&
Attire

At this point in your planning process, it is time for you to finalize the formality of your wedding, as you will soon need to convey this information to your guests so they can prepare accordingly. The formality of your wedding will, of course, depend on your venue and wedding style, taking into consideration any cultural or traditional aspects.

I want you to imagine your wedding as if it were a brand. You want the marketing materials (invitations, wedding website, etc.) to match the product (your wedding weekend). Every aspect of your planning should be dedicated to making your wedding formality a cohesive story.

There is no wrong or right way to go about choosing your personal attire and formality preference. Remember, it is your and your partner's day and the two of you get to decide what formality you want to have. Just make sure that you are communicating any attire and formality requirements with guests, so they can follow your guidelines. On the following pages, you will find suggestions on how to choose the attire and formality of your wedding.

❧ Deciding on the Dress Code ❧

Formality is most commonly defined by the dress code you choose for your wedding. However, it can also be defined through details such as flowers, place settings, whether you choose to do a buffet or sit-down dinner, and even the time of day in which you choose to have your wedding.

Let's refresh our memories on some basic, traditional dress codes before you choose one (or create one of your own!) for your wedding (see page 71). While these may not apply to your style of wedding, they may help kick-start your ideas on the formality you want to have on the day.

As I am sure you've noticed, some of these traditional dress codes can be very ambiguous and even overlap with each other in some cases. Dress codes are often an area of confusion for wedding guests as many people have different ways of interpreting them. Black-tie attire, for example, is relatively cut-and-dried, whereas formal attire is a bit more of a gray area.

TIP ❯ *If you are worried that your desired dress code is not clear, consider adding a guide with a clear description and photos to your wedding website to help direct your guests with what to wear so that it best fits the venue and your desired formality.*

There is a magic hour where day dress turns into evening dress, and that is 6 p.m. The more formal dress codes, especially black-tie attire, should only be designated for events that begin at 6 p.m. or later. Typically speaking, it would not be appropriate to have a black-tie or black-tie-optional wedding on a Sunday in the early afternoon.

TRADITIONAL DRESS CODES	DESCRIPTION	
Casual Attire ✳ *Be mindful that some people may interpret a casual dress code as being able to wear jeans.*	This can be a day dress or pants/skirt with blouse or a dress shirt and khaki pants.	
Cocktail Attire	This can be a short or mid-length cocktail dress or suit with tie.	
Semiformal Attire	This can be a cocktail or mid-length dress or suit with tie.	
Formal Attire ✳ *Be mindful that some people may interpret formal attire as synonymous with black-tie attire.*	This can be a floor-length or mid-length dress or suit with tie.	
Black-Tie Attire ✳ *Black-tie optional means your guests can dress in black-tie if they would like to, but it is not required.*	This can be a floor-length gown or tuxedo.	

The time of your event, venue, and dress code should be working together seamlessly to determine the overall formality of your wedding. As I mentioned, a black-tie wedding would need to occur after 6 p.m. To take that a step further and tie it all together, a black-tie wedding would also warrant a multi-course sit-down dinner. If your guests are dressing in black tie, they will be expecting a more formal venue and formal meal. That is truly how the three aspects work together. Now, you may be having a reception at a restaurant and choose to have a buffet-style dinner with everyone in cocktail attire. Those three aspects work together, too. Remember, these are not rules, but rather guidelines to help you decide on a few aspects of your big day that will contribute to the overall formality of your event. In the end, it has to fit your vision.

·» Choosing Wedding Attire «·

You've decided on the formality of your wedding. You've chosen what you would prefer your guests to wear. Now it's time to discuss the specifics of attire for everyone in the wedding. This includes you and your partner, your wedding party, and potentially immediate family.

Traditional-dress wearers, this first part will be specifically for you. What is one of the biggest decisions you will make for your wedding day? I bet it's something you have been dreaming about, if not planning for, for a big part of your life. Yes, I am referring to your wedding dress! It will be one of, if not the, most important and special outfits you will ever wear. (No pressure!) There are three main boxes to check in terms of the pre-work you'll want to do before shopping for the dream dress.

✤ COLLECTING INSPIRATION ✤

You can start this step as early in the planning process as you would like to, but may I just recommend you wait until you have the ring? This is where you let your creative juices flow and have fun discovering the elements, looks, and styles that speak to you. Think of it as your wedding dress vision board. It's a good place to start, and it will also help give your salesperson or store associates some direction on where to start based on what you like.

You may learn that you like a specific style, or designer, for example. Don't take this part too seriously; just have fun with it!

✤ CONSIDERING YOUR VENUE ✤

Before going shopping for your dress, you want to ensure your desired look is in line with your venue. Of course, this is your day, and you are free to do and wear whatever you please, but you may want to rule out certain styles or fabrics if you are having a beach wedding in eighty-degree weather, for example.

✤ REFERRING BACK TO YOUR BUDGET ✤

On page 26, we discussed all of the elements of creating your budget, and attire for you and your partner was part of that list. At this point in your planning process, revisit your budget to see if the number still remains the same. Set a number, or a range, that you can take with you on your shopping adventures.

TIP ❯ *If there is a specific designer that you adore, and their dresses fall somewhere in your budget, do some research to see if they are hosting a trunk show anywhere near where you live. Trunk shows will allow you to try on a range of dresses within this one designer's collection, and oftentimes you will be eligible for a discount if you choose to purchase one.*

✦ TIMELINE FOR BUYING A WEDDING GOWN ✦

For a traditional wedding gown, you will want to plan to purchase it nine to twelve months prior to your wedding day. The earlier the better to err on the side of caution. Seems early, doesn't it? That is because in most cases the dresses you try on in a traditional bridal salon are simply there for you as samples. Your actual dress may need to be ordered from the designer in your size, and shipped to the store you purchased it through.

The standard time for dress delivery at a traditional boutique is six to eight months once you order it. This is a long process! Again, this is a typical timeline, but it will differ depending on each individual store and designer. For this example, let's say you purchased your dress twelve months before your wedding and it arrived six months after you ordered it. That means that, in theory, there would be six more months until your wedding day. Within these six months, you will need to attend fitting appointments for alterations, pick out accessories, choose undergarments, and ultimately, take your dress home.

TIP ❯ *Pick out your shoes and undergarments prior to your fittings to ensure accuracy!*

Let's review this timeline:

- Nine to twelve months prior to wedding day: Shop for and purchase the dress.
- Six months prior to wedding day: Select undergarments, accessories, and shoes.
- Three to four months prior to wedding day: Confirm any alterations.
- Two to three weeks prior to wedding: Final fitting and dress pick-up.

Now, let's back up a bit and visit the part in your timeline where you begin shopping for and ultimately end up purchasing a dress. It's time to dive deeper into the actual shopping and appointment process, especially the challenges you might face. This applies to anyone shopping for a wedding outfit, no matter what that outfit might be. For starters, most bridal studios, or stores, do require appointments, so be sure to do your research, and prepare to book your visit in advance.

Etiquette tips to keep in mind for a happy and productive appointment:

- Arrive to your appointment on time.
- Come prepared with inspiration and a clear budget. You may end up loving something that differs from your inspiration, but at least you had somewhere to start!
- Respect the length of your appointment. Oftentimes, a bridal appointment will have a set duration.
- Ensure you are bringing people who will be supportive and respect the time and space, as they are a representation of you. You don't want to come out of the dressing room to see a family member looking through dresses in an area they were not permitted in.
- Don't get frustrated! Perhaps you just haven't found what you were looking for, or your salesperson is not as helpful as you'd hoped. Either way, be respectful and patient. If there is a serious issue, request to speak with a store manager.
- Don't forget to cancel future appointments elsewhere if you've found your dress at an earlier stop!

For those who are not wearing a traditional wedding gown and are going through that same process, it would still be smart for you to begin your shopping process six to eight months in advance to have plenty of time for special orders, alterations, etc. This can apply to cultural or religious attire as well as tuxedos, suits, or a less-traditional gown. If you have a partner who will be wearing a traditional tuxedo, that would fall under this ideal timeline as well.

❧ Wedding Party Attire ❧

On to the wedding party and their attire. Let's begin with timing; there is no standard timeline (unlike the wedding dress shopping process) for when exactly to have your wedding party order their gowns, suits, tuxedos, etc., but, the earlier the better!

As mentioned in the wedding party chapter, eight months is generally a good amount of time to give your wedding party plenty of notice for this role. If you are able to pick outfits six to eight months prior to the wedding, that would be ideal, so people can plan accordingly. You want to ensure there is enough stock available, and enough time for people to have their outfits altered if necessary. If you will be having flower girls or ring bearers and want to pick out or give guidance for their outfits, you can follow a similar timeline to the wedding party to keep yourself organized.

While you will obviously want to consider your wedding's formality, theme, colors, etc., the budget will most likely be the largest deciding factor when selecting outfits for your wedding party.

In the wedding party chapter, we discussed the importance of communicating the budget and financial responsibilities that your wedding party will have to take on. Out of respect for them and that discussion, it is imperative you find outfits that fall fairly within that decided budget, even if general numbers were thrown around early in the process.

When it comes to bridesmaids' dresses, there may be up to eight to ten different women of different shapes and sizes wearing the same style dress. With this in mind, you want to do your best to find a universally flattering design within your budget. Making everyone perfectly content will be nearly impossible, but you want to do your best to make sure your wedding party feels beautiful, confident, and comfortable in whatever they are wearing.

The last thing to keep in mind when it comes to picking out outfits for your wedding party is making sure your choices are appropriate and suitable for the venue, formality, and time of year. For example, a linen suit jacket would be more suitable for an outdoor beach wedding than it would be for an indoor wedding in a ballroom. Similarly, a plum velvet dress would make more sense for a fall or winter wedding than it would for a wedding in July. Not only will this look better visually, but choosing the right fabric for the time of year will keep your wedding party comfortable.

There are a few different ways to shop around for your wedding party attire. Some couples may choose to do all of their research online and send their wedding party a link for where to purchase or rent the items for their outfits. You may consider ordering the outfit to see it in-person and try it on yourself before making the final decision. Other couples may choose to set up an in-person shopping day with their wedding parties. This would allow the wedding parties to try on different options until the couple chooses their favorite. The method you end up choosing will be entirely up to you and your partner and may also depend on where your wedding party members are located geographically.

Your wedding party attire will contribute to the overall "brand" and formality of your wedding. While it won't be easy, it is important that you do everything in your power to balance getting the look you want with making sure your wedding party feels well put together and confident. Plus, you want everyone to look truly happy and comfortable in your wedding photographs, don't you?

—» ask mariah «—
Your Formality & Attire Questions

My partner and I are planning a special themed wedding and want our guests to dress in that theme. How do we make our dress code as stress-free as possible for our guests?

Creating a stress-free dress code means providing guests with as much clear information as possible. This would be a great time to take advantage of your wedding website (see the wedding website chapter), if you have one, by clearly explaining the theme and even adding photos to explain your desired dress code. In addition, you can add a small card to your invitation bundle with an explanation and even visuals. There is nothing wrong with asking your guests to dress in theme, but you want to take the guessing game out of it for them! Plus, this will ensure everyone (or most guests) comes dressed in the way you wish so your vision comes to life.

What is unacceptable to wear to a wedding in general? How can we communicate what is not acceptable at our wedding without offending anyone, especially older family members?

From a traditional standpoint, wearing white, red, and black dresses to weddings is often seen as no-no in some cultures. However, with all of the different wedding styles we see today, there are no additional global rules (other than what I've listed above) as to what is acceptable and unacceptable as it really depends on your wedding style. From an etiquette standpoint, it is much more polite to encourage guests on what they can wear rather than what they cannot. Similar to what we discussed about the themed wedding, you can utilize your wedding website to include photos that coincide with your dress code. This will come off a lot better than adding a bunch of pictures of what your guests should not wear.

My partner and I come from different cultures and we have different ideas for dress codes and traditional dress attire; how can we decide proper wedding attire?

The success story here will be a compromise! You may find that dressing in one traditional attire for the ceremony and one for the reception may work for you, or perhaps you each wear your own traditional attire and agree on a more universal dress code for your guests.

You may also want to consider which traditions from each of your cultures are important for your wedding and which you can compromise on so that you and your partner are able to represent your cultures.

Who should I bring with me to my shopping appointments?

The stores you plan to visit may have a policy on how many people are allowed to attend your shopping appointment. For this reason, you'll want to confirm that number for each place you shop before asking family members and friends to join you. You don't want to have to let anyone down or end up cutting back on people after the fact.

Within that number, you can invite anyone you'd like to come with you on your shopping trip. Just know that if four people accompany you on your appointment, that means four different opinions to digest with every outfit or dress you try on. Truly consider whose opinion you value when it comes to who you want there.

What if I have a very opinionated family member but I feel obligated to invite them to join the shopping trip?

Perhaps you have a very opinionated parent, but how could you NOT invite them to shop for your wedding dress? You will have to prepare yourself ahead of time for the inevitable comments and jabs. Ensure the rest of your guests are a strong support system, and just go back to the fact that it is your day.

Lean on the store employees, as they are experts in the field. Feel empowered to tell them the situation while you are in the dressing room, so they can best help you through it in the moment. This is not their first rodeo in dealing with difficult or opinionated family members, and having them do some of the heavy lifting may take the direct conflict out of the situation between you and your family member. It makes it feel less personal.

I fell in love with a dress/wedding outfit, but someone very close and important to me really does not like it. What do I do?

I have said this many times throughout this book: it is your wedding. You need to prioritize being happy and looking the way you desire on your wedding day over pleasing everyone. Don't underestimate the power of clear and intentional communication. If your sister is disagreeing with your choice as you stand in it, you must tell her how much you appreciate her opinion, and how honored you are that she is there with you to take part in this, but the dress you have on is the one that makes you feel most beautiful.

Odds are, your friend or family member just has your best interests in mind—after all, that is why you chose them to join you on the shopping trip. When in doubt, as I mentioned before, lean on your salesperson or store staff. They have had plenty of practice for this.

My partner is of a different faith/culture than me and they/their family want me to wear something traditional to the wedding, but I picture myself wearing something else. How do I honor their culture and traditions while also wearing something that I want and makes me feel comfortable and my best?

You, of course, should be wearing something on your wedding day that you are absolutely in love with. There are two main solutions you may want to consider to help honor your partner's culture and/or religion without compromising your dream wedding outfit. As discussed above, one option is to wear two different outfits: one for the ceremony and one for the reception. You may opt for a traditionally cultural or religious outfit for the ceremony to honor your partner and their family, then you can wear the outfit of your choice to the reception. Another option would be to wear the outfit of your choice, then accessorize with pieces that honor their religion or culture.

My fiancé and I are not having a traditional wedding; what can we wear to our wedding?

Anything that makes you feel like the most fabulous version of yourself on your most special and important day! You and your partner should choose whatever makes you feel comfortable—whether that be a dress, pant suit, tuxedo, or anything else. Keep in mind the formality of your wedding.

If I'm having two different ceremonies, is it appropriate to wear the same attire for both? Similarly, is it appropriate for me to change after the ceremony into something different for the reception?

It is entirely up to you! Do I sound like a broken record yet? This is a personal preference that also depends on what your budget allows and how traditional you want to be. You may find yourself wearing the same attire for multiple ceremonies and celebrations. You may also consider wearing something more traditional for a ceremony, then changing for the reception to wear something less traditional. It completely depends on your vision and wedding style.

If this is my second or third marriage, can I still wear white?

Not wearing white the second or third time around is a thing of the past! You can absolutely wear white to your wedding regardless of how old you are, or if this is your second or third wedding.

Is it appropriate for my partner and I to give our opinions on what our immediate family wears to our wedding?

You may find yourself being very hands-on with helping your immediate family select what they wear, or you may not. It will certainly be situational and dependent on individual relationships. It can be appropriate to give guidelines on what you would like everyone to wear to your wedding—they will likely be in many photographs, so it makes sense for you to care about what they wear. I would recommend keeping your guidelines quite vague, so your family members still feel empowered to wear something they feel sensational in. While it is your day, it is a very special day for them as well.

For example, you may suggest that they wear autumn colors (and provide a specific range of colors) to go along with your fall wedding. Or perhaps you ask them to wear something floral for your beach wedding. They will have something to follow, without feeling robbed of their individuality in the process. If you are in a position where you want to give them full freedom to wear whatever they would like, more power to you! However, it is not rude or inappropriate to allow your wishes to be heard.

How do I deal with a family member who is wearing something that I truly dislike or is potentially competing with/too similar to my wedding gown?

Wedding planning will bring up many stressors, and it is imperative that you pick and choose your battles. Be careful about offering up advice or opinions that were not asked of you, as you certainly do not want to rock any relationship boats through this process. If you are able to look past it and accept that it just may not be your style, but they really like it, that may be in your best interest.

Now, if you feel that someone is intentionally wearing something to try to compete with your dress, or perhaps to embarrass you, that is, of course, a separate issue. In this case, you may want to communicate with this person, gently saying that you hoped they wouldn't wear white on your wedding day, or perhaps that they would wear something other than a ball gown so similar to yours. While this conversation may be tricky and uncomfortable, you can offer to help them look for another option. Rest assured that you and your partner will be the star of your wedding day, as will your outfits.

What do I do if someone in my wedding party refuses to wear the outfit I chose for the wedding?

This is one of those things that you have to be up front about in the beginning with your chosen wedding party. While you may not know exactly what you want your wedding party to wear upon asking them to take on this role, you may consider having some inspiration prepared to show them such as pictures or a mood board and a budget in mind to give them an idea of what they are committing to. Nowadays, it is common that a bride may pick a bridesmaid dress that comes in different silhouettes and allow her bridesmaids to choose the silhouette they are most comfortable in. This is a great way to compromise as you will still be getting the look, color, and overall aesthetic that you want at your wedding, but your wedding party will feel empowered by choosing a style that flatters them most. If you communicate your intentions ahead of time and get an inclination that someone may be opposed to wearing something you are choosing for them, then you may have to have a conversation with them to see what may be causing them to oppose your outfit of choice and then try to come up with a compromise.

However, this ultimately depends on your individual situation and relationship with this person. If this person hasn't really been supportive and a compromise can't be made, then you may have to reconsider including them in your wedding party and perhaps honor them in some other way.

Wedding Preparation

At this point in your planning process, you've laid the groundwork. You've built a strong foundation by prioritizing the most time-sensitive aspects of planning and determining your high-level vision for your wedding day. Now it's time to get into the nitty-gritty details. We will use the foundation that you've built and start to fill in the missing pieces.

In this section, we will cover everything you need to know from wedding website etiquette to an in-depth guide to save-the-dates and invitations, to some of the exciting events that will take place leading up to the wedding, and more. You will find the answers to your questions about registries, rings, and accommodations, too. At the end of this section, I will also be providing tips and tricks for you to help you feel and appear like the most confident and polished version of yourself on your wedding day, and for every event leading up to it. Let's discuss the details.

Website

One of the aspects of etiquette that has fascinated and captivated me the most is how it evolves with the changing times. If you opened a wedding etiquette book from 1942, you might see sections dedicated to announcing your engagement, putting together your guest list, or even how to address your invitations. Sounds familiar, right? While some of the details will be different, the message and tradition will remain constant. However, I can confidently guarantee that this etiquette book from the 1940s will not have a section on whether or not it's appropriate to send an e-vite or the proper way to handle a wedding website!

Wedding websites act as a digital tool to help couples communicate their wedding plan details, offer necessary information for attendees, and even manage elements such as RSVPs and/or registries. They are used to enhance planning and communication, but they should not replace traditional invitations. While you may not note a specific detail about your wedding festivities in the invitation, such as the welcome party will be on the grass so it's best to wear an outdoor-friendly shoe, your wedding website would be the perfect place to include something like this.

✸ Creating a Website ✸

While wedding websites continue to become more and more common, whether or not to have one is entirely up to you and your partner. Simply speaking, having one should ultimately make your life and the lives of your guests easier. The key is to create a destination for your guests to have any of their questions answered (and not have to bother you with them!) while simultaneously giving you a platform to track and manage things digitally. Yes, there are several benefits to having one today, but successful weddings have occurred for many, many years without them, too.

Don't be surprised or frustrated if you have family members or friends who are skeptical of, or completely refuse to use, the wedding website. It is still a relatively new concept, and your wedding site may be the first one that some of your loved ones have come across. Offering a website as a feature to complement traditional communication without replacing it is what makes it a bonus feature for guests who choose to take advantage of it.

What should you include on your wedding website should you decide to have one? You may find that a few categories do not apply to you or you just don't want to include, as this will depend on your wedding style and preferences.

✦ YOUR LOVE STORY ✦

Your wedding website will be an extension of your entire celebration. Your guests will likely refer to it often when they receive the URL. You want to have a place to welcome them to the website and may consider a specific message, a brief description of your story, and some photos for the homepage.

✦ SCHEDULE ✦

You will want to create a tab or section that is dedicated to the different events that will take place over your wedding weekend. This is where you will include specific locations, times, dress codes, parking, and/or transportation details.

Your guests will appreciate you being as specific as possible, so they don't have to assume a certain outfit is correct, or whether or not transportation is provided for the reception.

✧ TRAVEL AND ACCOMMODATION ✧

You can note any hotel blocks you have reserved for your wedding weekend. Other accommodations in the area, local airports, and any transportation you are providing for events would also fit well here.

✧ REGISTRY ✧

Some wedding website platforms allow you to create a registry directly on your website. You can also include links to the different places where you are registered.

✧ THINGS TO DO IN THE AREA ✧

This part is especially important if you are having a destination wedding or if many of your guests are from out of town. You may consider listing some of your favorite restaurants, museums, sights, tours, and more for your guests to take advantage of in their free time while they are in town for your special weekend.

✧ WEDDING PARTY ✧

If you and your partner have chosen to have a wedding party, many couples will designate a tab to introduce their guests to the members of their wedding party with their pictures and names.

✧ RSVP ✧

Similar to the registries, some wedding websites also allow you to manage your RSVPs through the website. You may want to include a place for allergies, dietary restrictions, or special accommodations here. More on RSVP etiquette soon.

TIP ❯ *Having the option to RSVP via the website in addition to, instead of replacing, physical RSVP cards is one of the ways you can offer traditional communication for guests who are not completely comfortable with using wedding websites.*

❖ PHOTOS ❖

This is optional, of course, but you may want to dedicate a section of your site to a gallery of photos from your relationship for an extra personal touch.

❖ SOCIAL MEDIA/TECHNOLOGY GUIDELINES ❖

If you prefer for guests not to take photographs during the ceremony or reception and/or post any photographs on social media, your website would be a good place to note that.

TIP ❯ *You could also add any health guidelines to your website if you and your partner deem it appropriate or if you, your partner, or any guests are immunocompromised.*

Using a platform that is specifically created for you to curate your dream wedding website is the most user-friendly route to take. There are many different sites in existence that offer this service. They will hold your hand through the process and ensure you are not missing any of the necessary steps. They are made to handle exactly what you are using your website for, whether that is strictly for communication or to also manage your registry and responses.

TIP ❯ *You can notify your guests that you have a wedding website through your save-the-dates, wedding invitation, and/or shower invitation. It is acceptable to put a URL directly on a save-the-date or shower invitation, but it is not customary to add a URL to a formal wedding invitation. If you want to include a URL with your invitation, you may want to add a small card with the information to accompany the actual invitation. More on save-the-dates and invitations to come.*

—» ask mariah «—
Your Wedding Website Questions

How do we relay all of our wedding information included on the website to people who are not comfortable with or able to access our website for whatever reason?

Remember, while helpful and efficient, your wedding website should not be replacing an invitation sent with the necessary information. A website is completely optional, so it should not be your only source of information for your guests. If you know of a specific guest who will not be comfortable accessing the website or may be unable to access it for a reason such as age or disability, you may ask a family member, another guest close to them, a member of your wedding party, or perhaps even you or your partner to lend a helping hand to ensure they have all of the necessary information.

TIP ➤ Make sure that your site is organized and easily digestible, so it is as accessible as possible for your guests. Be mindful of the colors, fonts, and methods you use to relay your information, such as adding captions to videos. If you and/or your partner's family are bilingual, it may be good to add translations to the information on your website.

How can we prevent strangers or uninvited guests from accessing our website with all of our wedding information?

You may want to consider protecting your website with a password to prevent strangers from accessing it. You may also want to politely communicate on your website that you would appreciate if your guests kept the URL private. You could say something like "Please kindly do not share our wedding website with anyone outside our guest list. Thank you!"

Registry

Can you remember a time when you were quite young, circling items in a catalog that you wanted Santa to bring you for Christmas or for your family to buy you for the holidays? I have good news! You have a chance to do this again as an adult. While your favorite childhood toys will be replaced with a KitchenAid mixer, a new set of bed sheets, or your most desired glassware, the process will be an ode to your childhood holiday wish list.

At this point in your process, it will be just about time to create your registry if you plan to have one. It is a good thing to do in conjunction with creating your wedding website, should you choose to have one. Your registry will be a list of items, specifically curated by you, that you would want to receive as shower or wedding gifts. The original purpose of a wedding registry was for a couple to collect items to help them move into their first home. While times have certainly changed, and every couple's living situation at the time of getting married will differ, the idea is that your registry list will help you fill your home with things you may need as a couple. Your guests may use your registry to purchase items for your shower or wedding, but some may not refer to it at all.

❧ Creating a Registry ❦

How do you know where to register or what to register? This is a completely personalized process! Your registry should be filled with a fair balance between needs and wants. After all, it's really just an adult wish list. Begin by creating a list of things you need as a couple. These could be small kitchen appliances, glassware, silverware, full place settings, linens, etc. Once you have completed this, you can start to come up with your wants.

Some common places that you may want to consider for your registry are various department stores, home goods stores, and/or furniture stores. If you choose to utilize a wedding website, some of them allow you to create your registry directly through the website platform.

❧ A Honeymoon Fund ❦

In this day and age, it is absolutely acceptable to add a honeymoon fund to your registry or have that in place of a registry. Some couples may find themselves living together for many years before marriage, which can mean they already have many of the items you would find on a typical registry. Others just may not be interested in receiving physical gifts. While upgrading your current items is always an option, some may prefer to collect money for a honeymoon instead. Is it really as tacky as some people believe it to be? If it is not worded or presented correctly, it certainly can be!

So, use verbiage such as, "If you are able to give, we have chosen a honeymoon fund in lieu of (or as an alternative option to) physical gifts." Additionally, you will want to use a honeymoon fund platform or website rather than collecting money through a money collection app or website. You are probably asking yourself, "Is there really a difference?" Technically, there is not, but using a platform makes it a bit more tasteful, and people will feel as if they are really contributing to a specific gift that you are asking for in the same way as purchasing something off of a registry. It's all about your delivery. Many wedding websites will offer a way to add your honeymoon fund directly to your registry, so it appears seamlessly as an additional gift option that your guests can contribute to.

On this note, while I believe honeymoon funds are absolutely acceptable, having a general money collection fund is not something I would recommend when looking at it through an etiquette lens. You will certainly have people who choose to give you money in the form of a check or cash as a wedding gift, but asking for it directly can come off as poor taste.

Making Guests Aware of
✯ Your Registry ✯

It is considered a faux pas to put any specific registry information on a formal wedding invitation. In past times, people were made aware of a wedding registry through word of mouth. It is acceptable to note the information on a wedding shower invitation, however, or you can choose to add an extra card of information in the main invitation envelope. If you choose to use a wedding website, simply making your guests aware of the URL as with the save-the-date will give them early access to your registry without offense. If you are not having a shower or using a wedding website, I would recommend mailing or emailing the information to notify guests.

Do not be surprised if guests choose to give you a physical gift that does not live on your registry, or simply to give money. Your guests are not required to shop from your registry. Plus, you may have some guests who are not comfortable shopping on a registry website and prefer to pick out something of their own.

TIP ❯ *Avoid sharing your registry information on social media, via text or email, or putting it directly on your wedding invitation.*

—» ask mariah «—
Your Wedding Registry Questions

How should I determine what the least expensive item on my registry is versus the most expensive item?

Many registries allow people to contribute to gifts without having to purchase them in their entirety. This takes a lot of pressure off your guests, so it is perfectly acceptable to put a few higher-cost items on there. You want to have a good range of prices throughout the registry to give your guests options. Focus more on including things you truly want and need. Your guests will contribute what they are able to.

Should we expect to receive the actual gifts at our shower or wedding?

The etiquette around gift-giving for showers is to either bring the gift or mail it to their home. For the actual wedding, the proper etiquette is to never arrive at the ceremony or reception with a physical gift, but a monetary gift would be acceptable. A card with money inside is appropriate, but walking in with a blender is not. You will have the opportunity to add your mailing address to the registry, and because of this, you should expect to receive gifts at your home shortly after you've given out your wedding website or put the places where you are registered on your shower invitation. Depending on where you choose to register, they may also offer the option to send one complete delivery once the list is closed.

TIP ❯ *Make sure you designate a place at your reception where people can leave cards. Many guests will bring money in a card as your wedding gift, and you don't want them to have to come to you to ask where to leave it. In addition, be prepared in case there is that one guest that does bring a physical gift. Clearly signpost this space or assign someone to be responsible for doing this, such as someone who works at the venue or someone in your wedding party.*

it typical to receive a gift for the shower but not the wedding?

is customary for gifts to be given by guests for both the shower and the edding. Many times, guests invited to the shower will purchase a gift from e registry and then give a monetary gift on the wedding day. While this is istomary, do not take it personally if someone is giving as much as they can, hich may be one gift from the registry.

am over fifty and this is not my first wedding. Should I have a registry?

here is nowhere that says you shouldn't! Regardless of how your first wedding anned out, it should not dim the light on your second or even your third edding. Your wedding is still a wedding regardless of your age or past. You psolutely should make a registry if you want or need things. People will give hat they are able to. If you do not feel comfortable creating a registry at this age of your life, the alternatives listed below may apply to you.

hat if we don't want to have a registry or ask for gifts at all?

is your wedding, after all! You can note on your website, shower invitation, r wedding invitation that you do not want to receive gifts. Something along e lines of "Your presence is enough. No gifts, please" will work well. If you el called to, you can note that you would like your guests to donate to a harity of your or their choosing in lieu of gifts.

IP ❯ *In general, if any invitation notes "no gifts," the proper etiquette in this situation is to respect the hosts' wishes and not bring a gift. You will have people who will insist on bringing something anyway, so be prepared with thank-you notes just in case. More on that soon.*

Save-
the-
Dates

Wait! Before you move forward with reading this section, your guest list must be ticked and tied. Why? Because anyone who receives a save-the-date receives an invitation to your wedding. Plain and simple. This includes plus-ones, too, so you want to ensure your envelopes are addressed properly.

The purpose of a save-the-date is exactly what it sounds like it would be for—for people to mark the date in their calendars! You are notifying everyone on your guest list of the date and location you have chosen for your wedding. The save-the-date can be sent out by the couple or by the hosts. The information should be clear and minimal, and your guests should receive more information through the invitation and/or wedding website. There are no "rules" for how a save-the-date should be designed or worded, but there are a few things you will want to include. Your save-the-dates should be sent out at least six to eight months prior to your wedding day. If you are having a destination wedding, it would be safe to send them out at least nine to twelve months prior.

What Should Be Included
⟫ on Your Save-the-Date? ⟪

Here is a list of what you should be including in your save-the-dates:

- Your wedding date(s).

- The general location (you do not need to disclose the exact venue at this time; the city/town will suffice for the purpose of the save-the-date, and people can learn more about the specific venue through your wedding website, if you are having one).

- Wedding website URL (if you are using one).

- A photo of you and your partner (optional, of course).

- Some type of verbiage that leads your guests to learn that a formal invitation will follow.

TIP ❯ *Also, if you are having multiple events throughout the weekend, or you are having a destination wedding, be sure to include the relevant series of dates, or use "save the weekend" verbiage.*

Your save-the-dates are a great way to get the word out about your wedding early. It gives you the chance to make sure your guests mark the date in their calendar, share your wedding website, and get the excitement buzzing around the whole event. Whether you choose to send your save-the-date digitally, make it yourself, or have a stationer create it, the reason why you send it remains the same. Next come the invitations.

✧ SAVE-THE-DATES EXAMPLES ✧

As I mentioned, there are no rules for exactly how to design or word your save-the-dates. You can be as formal or as casual as you want to be as long as you include the basic information needed (see list above). I've provided two general examples on the following page that you can use to begin crafting your own.

Traditional Style:

X (enter name) & X (enter name) are getting married!
Enter date (e.g., June 14, 2024)
Miami, Florida
Please see further wedding details:
Enter URL
Formal invitation to follow.

Weekend Verbiage:

Save the weekend!
X and X are getting hitched!
Enter dates (e.g., June 14, 2024 – June 16, 2024)
Riviera Maya, Mexico
Please see further wedding information at:
Enter URL
Invitation to follow.

QUESTIONS TO ASK BEFORE WORKING
✧ ON YOUR SAVE-THE-DATES ✧

Do you have your wedding guest list confirmed?	Yes or No
Have you and your partner confirmed your wedding date?	Yes or No
Do you have the location confirmed?	Yes or No
If you are including a wedding website, do you have it up and running?	Yes or No
Are you having multiple events that you need to make sure to communicate?	Yes or No

—» *ask mariah* «—
Your Save-the-Date Questions

Can we send our save-the-date digitally?

Absolutely! This is your wedding, and remember this book is filled with advice to help you, not rules to hinder you. You are free to do as you please. Sending a digital save-the-date or invitation will certainly be less formal than a mailed one, so just refer back to your overall "wedding brand" in terms of formality when considering this. If you choose to send them via mail, the next chapter on invitations will give you everything you need to know about addressing the envelopes.

Are save-the-dates required?

They are not—again, no rules. You may find yourself having a very short engagement where time does not allow for both a save-the-date and an invitation. If you do have a date set that is further out, or you are having a destination wedding, it is helpful to send them out in some form so that people do not double-book themselves. You want as many of your loved ones as possible to be able to attend your very special event!

Should we expect to receive RSVPs after sending out a save-the-date?

An RSVP should not be requested on a save-the-date, nor is it required. Do not plan to truly account for people attending until you send out formal invitations. With that being said, there will be guests who may let you know that they are unable to attend for whatever reason upon receiving the save-the-date.

Do we need to send an invitation to someone who told us they are not able to attend after sending out save-the-dates?

Yes, yes, yes! Your guest list is your guest list. It would not be proper etiquette to not send them the invitation. For what it's worth, their plans may have changed, and they are able to attend. Send everyone on your guest list an invitation, too.

How do we tactfully reach out to our guests to get their mailing address for save-the-dates and invitations?

Address books seem to be a thing of the past for many. Your first step should be utilizing family, close friends, and your wedding party to collect as many addresses as you can! They will most likely have a running list for previous engagements and holiday cards. To fill in the gaps, create a beautiful digital flyer online that you can email and text people that states your request for their mailing address. This will be more exciting and creative than just sending out a typical email or text.

What is the best way to send "save-the-dates" if we are having two or more ceremonies/celebrations?

If you are inviting each guest to all of the celebrations, you may want to make a save-the-date card with each event clearly listed. That way it is communicated from the start, and people can begin to mark their calendars and prepare. If you are inviting different guests to the multiple ceremonies and celebrations, it would probably be most efficient to make a small card for each event and send each person/couple/family an envelope that includes the save-the-dates for the events they are invited to.

It will be best to aim to send everything out at the same time, so guests are setting proper expectations and you avoid unintentionally hurting anyone's feelings. This will take some extra time and focus for sure, but it will keep you organized if your guest list differs from event to event. The only exception to this would be if a certain celebration is taking place at a much later date.

How do we make "save-the-dates" written in multiple languages not feel overbearing?

If you are sending physical cards, consider taking advantage of the front and back to include more than one language. If using an electronic format, it might be easiest to make two different versions of the same save-the-date design and send the appropriate version to each guest. Or if creating two different versions feels overwhelming, you can stick to one version and try to fit everything in as best as possible.

Invitations

This chapter will be the most technical of them all, as invitations require a lot of careful attention. Not to worry, though; upon reading this section you will feel empowered and prepared to approach this part of your planning process head-on! If you plan to use a stationery designer, I highly suggest choosing one whom you really trust to help you get the job done. If you choose to do them yourself, don't be afraid to call in your wedding party or family for help. Now, this poses the question: are digital wedding invitations tacky?

I will repeat what I wrote in the previous chapter: they must match the formality of your wedding. While a digital invitation can be acceptable for certain styles of weddings, I recommend an old-fashioned invitation mailed right to your guests' homes. Mailed wedding invitations are one of those traditions that you probably want to consider keeping. The consistency of them over decades guarantee clear communication, organization, and respect for both you and your guests. We don't want to fix something that isn't broken!

❧ Timeline of Invitations ❧

Let's discuss the timeline. Remember, your save-the-dates should be sent out six to eight months prior to your wedding day, and with even more notice for a destination wedding. As for wedding invitations, eight to twelve weeks prior to your wedding day is a safe standard to stick to. For destination weddings, the earlier the better.

Now you may be thinking, oh good, we have all the time in the world! While this is one component of your planning process that may seem like it comes together closer to the actual day, the design process, printing, stuffing, and mailing will end up taking you quite some time.

If you are choosing to work with a company, my recommendation is to have the invitations ordered at least six months in advance, which means the design process is completed by this time and they are ready to be sent to the printer. You want to ensure you check, recheck, and then triple-check all the wording and spelling on your invitations and envelopes before they are sent to the printer, whether you are doing them yourself or outsourcing them.

What Usually Accompanies
❧ an Invitation ❧

If you've received a wedding invitation before, you know there is usually more to it than just a single-sheet invitation. There are a few components that may make up the stuffed envelope in its entirety, which are in addition to the actual wedding invitation. Please note that each component is technically optional for reasons that will be explained on the following pages.

❖ RSVP CARD OR RESPONSE CARD ❖

Historically, if an RSVP card was not provided, guests would send a handwritten letter indicating whether or not they were able to attend a wedding. Having an RSVP card is the most common and traditional way to manage replies. You can opt to have guests RSVP digitally via email or text if you would like to save money on stationery, or if you find that easier to manage. If you choose to go this route, you would not include an RSVP card with the invitation, but rather note on the invitation that responses are being collected via email, text, or your wedding website. Again, just keep in mind the formality of your wedding, and how your invitation bundle can best represent it. I would recommend having a physical RSVP card if you are able to. We will talk about RSVPs in more detail later in this chapter.

Proper verbiage for response cards:

RSVP

M _____

_____ *Accepts*

_____ *Declines*

Kindly reply by (enter date)

What to Add to a Response Card:

- Often times, you will see an "M" followed by a blank line where the guest would indicate their social title, such as Mr., Ms., or Mx. You can choose to include the "M" or you may want to consider putting a blank line only for people to write their title and/or name as they choose.

- This card is where you will indicate your required response date.

- If you are having people choose a dinner option ahead of time, you can list the options for them to check off.

- You may also want to consider having a space for someone to indicate a food allergy or dietary restriction that they may have.

- Typically, a response is not required for a ceremony but it is for a reception. Therefore, an invitation that is for both a ceremony and a reception would typically require an RSVP.

- You can simply put the abbreviation "RSVP" in the bottom left, which stands for "répondez s'il vous plaît," which translates to "respond if you please," or "please respond." Writing "RSVP please" would be redundant. You can also opt for "Please respond."

- If you are not taking the route of a traditional response card and are choosing to collect responses via a wedding website or digitally, you can still have a separate piece of stationery that reads something similar to this: "Kindly reply via our wedding website by (X date): (enter website here)." If this is the route you decide to take, make sure the wedding website form includes the necessary points listed above in some way, such as a space for their name, required response date, food choice (if needed), and a space to list allergies.

TIP ❯ *Ensure the response is accompanied by a pre-addressed and stamped envelope so your guests can return it with ease.*

✧ RECEPTION CARD ✧

The purpose of a reception card is to invite guests to a reception that is separate from the ceremony. This would apply to a private ceremony for family only, for example. Those who are invited to attend both events would receive the ceremony invitation in addition to the reception card, where those who are only invited to the reception will only receive the reception card. For this reason, you may want your reception card to mimic the look of an invitation so it is presented well to those only invited to the reception. If you are having a ceremony that leads right into a reception, or a ceremony where all guests are invited, you will not need to have a reception card as everything can go together on the main invitation.

An example of proper verbiage for a reception card in a situation where a ceremony invitation is also included:

A reception will follow the ceremony at Red Hawk Country Club
123 Oak Drive
Seven o'clock
RSVP

✤ ACCOMMODATION CARD ✤

If you have hotel blocks or designated accommodation for your wedding weekend, you can include a card of information along with your invitation bundle. If you've already put the information on your wedding website, this can be optional. If you do not have a wedding website, this would be the best method of notifying your guests of this information.

An example of proper verbiage for accommodation card:

Accommodation:
A block of rooms has been reserved at The Waverly Inn for your convenience
9 Waverly Place
917-432-6750
Please make your reservations before December 5th.
There will be a bus to transport guests from the hotel to the ceremony. The bus will be leaving The Waverly Inn promptly at 4:45 p.m. The bus will leave from the reception at 9:30 p.m. and 11 p.m. to take guests back to the hotel.

More details can be found on our wedding website here: (enter website).

✤ THE INVITATION ✤

Now, let's discuss that actual invitation. This is a page you'll want to bookmark! Next, you will find some examples of proper verbiage for your invitations to help guide you through creating yours. There will be a variation of wording, situations, and specifics that you can use as a reference. Later, there will also be a guide for properly addressing envelopes for you to reference.

✦ THE SKELETON OF A FORMAL INVITATION ✦

Here are the basic things to include in an invitation:

- Who is hosting?
- What is the purpose of the event? (Marriage, reception, etc.)
- Who is the event honoring? (Add the couple's names.)
- When is the event taking place?
- Where is the event taking place?
- What is the dress code?
- RSVP verbiage if applicable.

While using proper verbiage on your invitations and properly addressing the envelopes are traditions you will want to stick to, the size and style of your invitations are things you can and should have fun with. This is a perfect place to add your wedding branding and style. Your guests should be able to get a feel for the formality and style of your wedding through the type of invitation you choose. Of course, adding bells and whistles will come with an extra cost, but there is still plenty you can do with font, color, and layout to get your desired branding and formality across without spending a fortune.

Historically, the traditional size for a wedding invitation was 4.5 by 6.25 inches. More common now is the 5 by 7 inch invitation. A traditional response card would be 3 by 5 inches, and there is no standard size for an accommodation or reception card, as it will depend on what you would like to include on those, should you choose to have them. While these sizes are standard and traditional, there is no rule that says you must send an invitation that is of a certain size or shape.

If you are working with a wedding invitation designer, you may want to consider other printed items for your wedding along the same theme as your invitation. Here is a brief list to refer to when you are meeting with your invitation team:

- Ceremony programs
- Dinner menus
- Ceremony or reception signs
- Seating cards and seating chart
- Welcome letters for hotel guests

- A guest book
- Personal stationery
- Thank-you notes
- Shower invitations

✤ PROPER INVITATION VERBIAGE EXAMPLES ✤

→ **When one member of the couple's parents are hosting:**

(Enter titles and the full name of one or both parents—
e.g., Mr. and Mrs. Ryan Smith or Mrs. Beth Smith and Mrs. Maria Peters)
Request the pleasure of your company at the marriage of their child
(Enter full name—e.g., Brittany Smith)
to
(Enter full name—e.g., Grant Peters)
Saturday, the twenty-second of April (two thousand twenty-three)
At five o'clock
The Ritz-Carlton Philadelphia
10 Avenue of the Arts
Reception to follow
Black Tie
RSVP

*Note: Listing the year is optional, but if you do, it's best to write it out.

—→ **When both sets of parents are hosting together:**

(Enter titles and full name of one or both parents—
e.g., Doctor and Mrs. Timothy Silver)
and (Enter titles and full name of one or both parents—
e.g., Mr. and Mrs. James Freidman)
Request the honor of your presence at the marriage of their children
(Enter full name) and (Enter full name)
Friday, the eighth of September
At six o'clock
Uptown Community Church
551 Fort Washington Avenue, New York City
Cocktail attire

(This is an example of an invitation that would have a reception card. Typically, there is no RSVP verbiage needed because it is a ceremony invitation. Continue reading for an example of proper reception card verbiage.)

—→ **When family members who are not parents are hosting the wedding:**

(Enter title and full name of person 1—e.g., Doctor Elizabeth Stratton)
and (Enter title and full name of person 2—e.g., Mr. Philip Stratton)
Request the pleasure of your company at the marriage of their family member
(Enter full name)
to
(Enter full name)
Etc.

—→ **When either partner's parents are divorced but are hosting together (same last names, neither party is remarried):**

(Enter title and full name—e.g., Mrs. Ingrid White)
and (Enter title and full name—e.g., Mr. Craig White)
Request the honor of your presence at the marriage of their child
Etc.

→ **When you and your partner are hosting the wedding:**

Enter your or your partner's full name) and (Enter your or your partner's name)
Request the honor of your presence to witness their marriage to each other
Etc.

→ **A less-formal option in which parents are hosting:**

(Enter titles and full name of one or both parents)
Invite you to join them in celebration of the marriage between
(Enter full name) and (Enter full name)
Saturday, October 9th, 2022, at 5 p.m.
Graystone Catering
Old Bridge, New Jersey
Reception to immediately follow

→ **A less-formal option in which the couple is hosting:**

We are saying "I do!"
Please join us to celebrate our marriage
(Enter your or your partner's full name) and
(Enter your or your partner's full name)
Etc.
(You can include your wedding website URL here.)

→ **An invitation to the reception only:**

(Enter titles and full name of one or both parents)
Request the pleasure of your company
At the wedding reception for their child
(Enter full name)
and (Enter full name)

TIP ❯ *Remember, specific registry information should not be listed on the actual invitation. The words on your invitation should be centered, except for your RSVP verbiage. The RSVP verbiage should be placed on the bottom left of the invitation, and only invitations to the reception or both the ceremony and the reception.*

How to Properly Address
⋄» an Envelope «⋄

Here is a a refresher for how to properly address an envelope.

Social title refresher:

Miss: Used for ladies under the age of eighteen.

Ms.: Used for ladies over the age of eighteen who are unmarried, or for those whom you do not know their marital status. Ms. can also be used for divorced women regardless of whether or not their last name remains the same. This is typically a safe bet if you are ever unsure.

Mrs.: Married or widowed women.

Mr.: Used for all men, whether or not they are married.

Mx.: For guests who are gender neutral or gender fluid.

TIP ❯ *If you are unsure which social title someone prefers, it is acceptable to write out their full name without this information. Also, if you know one of your guests uses a professional title such as Dr., it is most respectful to use that on your invitation envelope. For instance, Dr. Alana Marks and Mr. Frederick Marks, or Dr. and Mrs. Bradley Kraft.*

When addressing an envelope to an entire family, you can simply write out "The
_ Family." When someone is invited with a plus-one, it would read as "Title/Full
_ame and Guest." Lastly, if you have guests who live together but are unmarried,
t may look something like this: "Ms. Morgan Drake and Mr. Kyle Matthews."
n this specific example, the lady's name is written first out of respect.

TIP ❯ _When wording invitations and addressing envelopes, you want
to write out everything to match the formality of the invitation. For
example, it should read "Saturday, the 27th of June" instead of "June
27th." Similarly, you want to address envelopes without abbreviations.
So you would write 123 Main Street instead of Main St. You would also
write out New York instead of NY._

The Proper Order for
⋅❯ Stuffing Envelopes ❮⋅

And for the last step before sending them off: What is the proper order to
tuff your envelopes in? The most important thing to remember here is that
ou want all the words facing the correct way when your guests go to open the
nvitation. There is no true, "proper" order to use when it comes to stuffing
our envelopes. It should be visually appealing, so if there is one guideline to
ollow it is to lay the components one on top of each other in size order. Place
he response card under the flap of its accompanying envelope. If you choose
o use an inner envelope in addition to the main envelope, leave it unsealed.
'he outer envelope will be fully addressed to the guests with their names and
ddress, where the inner envelope would contain only their names. Tissue
aper is sometimes used to lay flat in between each component to prevent
ny ink from smudging.

Your Invitations Questions

Who should mail the invitations?

Your wedding invitations should include a return address that belongs to whoever is hosting your wedding. The person who actually puts them in the mail is completely up to you. Now, this doesn't mean you can't help with the stuffing and mailing if your family is hosting the wedding. If you and your partner are hosting the wedding, the return address will be yours.

What is the best way to manage RSVPs?

When it comes to managing RSVPs, there is one method I recommend using that will work regardless of how you decide to collect responses. If you choose to have a wedding website, some platforms allow for you to offer guests the opportunity to RSVP directly through the site. You may consider offering this in addition to or in place of RSVP cards. You also may only be requesting responses via text or email. Or perhaps you are doing it the old-fashioned way with response cards only. Regardless of the method(s) you choose, I recommend using your original guest list spreadsheet. You can either add an extra column to indicate a yes or no, or highlight them in certain colors to indicate their response. You can also utilize your spreadsheet to mark down a food allergy that comes through with the reply. This method will keep you organized, and you will already have the groundwork laid for you from your master list that you created from the very beginning.

Our RSVP date has passed, and we still have quite a few guests that haven't responded. How do we handle this situation?

In any instance where a guest has not responded to an invitation when a response was required, regardless of the type of event, it is up to the host to reach out. In the case of your wedding, an RSVP is crucial as you, your venue, and your vendors will be awaiting a final count for purposes such as seating, food, etc. Whoever is hosting your wedding—whether it be a family member or you and your partner—one of you will have to contact those guests whose RSVPs are missing. It is important that you wait until after the RSVP date to give them the benefit of the doubt. Here is an example of the verbiage you may want to use. This may differ, of course, depending on your relationship, or your hosts' relationship with them.

Hello, (insert name)! I hope you are doing well.
I have not received your response to (our or the couple's names) wedding yet,
and I am reaching out in hopes you are able to join us for the festivities!

What if someone RSVPs and then later says they can't make it? How do we handle this?

Unfortunately, this is not uncommon. If it is early enough in the process, it is usually not the end of the world. If it happens at the last minute and you are having a wedding with a seated meal, it would be best to notify your venue that your number has changed. If your wedding is cocktail-party style, it may not make a difference. Next, you may need to make adjustments, such as your seating chart. I would advise against taking this as an opportunity to invite someone to take their place. As I mentioned when we discussed guest lists, you do not want anyone to feel like they were an afterthought or on the "B List."

What is the best way to notify our venue of all of the food allergies that come through in our guests' responses?

Firstly, it is important to note the difference between a true food allergy or dietary restriction and a preference. Your venue will certainly not be able to accommodate everyone's preferences. You will want to deliver this information to your venue once you have a seating chart completed. That way, the staff will know exactly where your guests with specific allergies and dietary restrictions are seated. If you are having a buffet, it would be best to try to include a variety of options and put information in front of each tray about what that dish contains, or what may be nut free, dairy free, etc.

Accommodation
&
Transportation

Whether you are having a destination wedding, a hometown wedding, or something in between, you may want to consider organizing accommodation for your guests. Even if you are having a local wedding, you will most likely have guests who are from out of town or who live far enough away that they will not want to drive home after the festivities.

First and foremost, you will want to consider different options for accommodation, if you have that ability based on your location. This will allow your guests to make a decision on where to stay based on where they are comfortable financially. It will show your guests that you put a lot of thought into making sure they are taken care of during your special weekend. When considering these options, try to keep in mind the distance from the venue, price, safety, accessibility, services provided, and type of accommodation (rental condo, hotel room, motel room, etc.). You may find yourself limited to one particular hotel and/or motel based on your wedding's location.

❧ Hotel Blocks ❧

If you've found a hotel(s) that will work well for your guests, the next step would be to book a hotel block(s). This is simply a certain number of rooms at a particular hotel that are "reserved" by you through the hotel at no cost to you, which will be available for your guests to book at a discounted price. When your guests book their rooms, they will mention your name or special code to receive the agreed-upon rate. It is best to book your hotel blocks as early as possible (at least eight months prior) to ensure the hotel is available to accommodate your number of guests.

Be sure to ask your hotel appropriate questions before deciding to block or book rooms. Some example questions include: How many rooms can I block? Is there a cutoff date for my blocked rooms to be booked? What amenities do you offer? What services do you have for disabled guests? Do you offer transportation? Are there any discount rates for booking/blocking rooms?

❧ Transportation ❧

The last thing you will want to consider regarding transportation and accommodations for your guests is whether or not you will be providing a transportation method during your wedding festivities. This, of course, is optional and will depend on how far your accommodation options are from the actual wedding. You may offer a bus service to the venue from one of your hotels. It may make sense to offer transportation at your wedding depending on location and whether or not your guests require special accommodations.

As this will be an additional expense, you will have to decide if your individual wedding calls for it, and if there was any money set aside in your budget for something like this. If you will be providing any kind of transportation, you can include the specifics on a tab or section on your wedding website or on the information card with the invitation. Transportation will be especially important if you have a destination wedding, as most likely guests will not know much about the location.

–» ask mariah «–
Your Accommodation Questions

How do we make our guests aware of the accommodation details or hotel blocks?

This is where your wedding website will come in handy! In the wedding website chapter we discussed designating a special tab on your website for travel and accommodation information. If you will not be having a wedding website, you can include an information card with your invitation as stated in the save-the-dates chapter.

How can we add a special, personal touch to the accommodation we selected for our guests?

A small welcome gift bag could be a wonderful option! When your guests check into the designated accommodation they will receive this welcome gift specially curated by you. You can fill the bag with items that are local to the area where you are having your wedding, any kind of snacks or drinks, a map of the area, a personalized welcome letter, a wedding weekend itinerary reminder, etc. Anything goes here, and you can be as creative as you want! Now, don't worry if a full gift bag is not in your budget; a welcome letter with an itinerary in a beautiful envelope is still a wonderfully thoughtful gesture that your guests will appreciate. Remember we discussed your "wedding brand" in the formality and attire chapter? This is a great opportunity for you to incorporate your branding and colors, whether you choose to do the gift bag, welcome letter, or both!

What is the proper etiquette for paying for hotel accommodation?

Your guests will be fully responsible for paying for their own accommodation. If budget allows, you'll sometimes find that the couple or hosts contribute to or pay for the wedding party to stay together, but that would be the only exception.

Rings

Let's talk about the very symbol of your marriage to your partner: your wedding bands! This will be the last non-event planning aspect we discuss for your wedding. There are two key planning points to keep in mind when it comes to the rings, and that is when to purchase them and what to do with them on the day of your wedding.

Where both partners may not have been involved in choosing an engagement ring, the shopping process for the wedding bands usually looks a little different. Typically, an engaged couple will go together to pick out their wedding bands. The reason why is, traditionally speaking, each partner (or their family) would purchase the other partner's ring for them. While how you choose to pay for the rings will depend on your individual budget and financial preferences as a couple, it can and should still be something you do together.

❋ Timing for Purchasing Rings ❋

You can plan for an exciting date day or date night as a way to take a break from the stresses of wedding planning, and truly make it a special moment to celebrate as a couple. After all, it is the very symbol of the vow you are going to be making to each other in the near future. In terms of timing, it is recommended that you pick out your wedding bands at least three to four months prior to your wedding day. This gives enough wiggle room for any issues that may arise and allows you to have them in your hands well before the actual wedding day.

TIP ❯ *Do you want to have your rings photographed before the ceremony? Be sure to coordinate this ahead of time so the correct person is giving the photographer the rings and taking them back. You want there to be clear communication so you do not need to worry during the day of.*

❋ Picking the Right Ring for You ❋

Ring shopping can feel like a high-pressure job. Since you will be wearing this ring for a better part of the rest of your life, it is important to choose a ring that is both special and practical for your lifestyle. So, while it might be one more thing added to your to-do list, you may want to spend time and effort finding your rings.

Before you go ring shopping, set a budget and stick to it. While it is important to pick a ring you love, it's also important to stay within your budget. It is likely that you came up with a rough number when first creating your overall budget. At this point, you'll want to finalize the number so you can give your jeweler realistic expectations at the beginning of your shopping experience.

Be sure to work with a reputable jeweler to ensure you are choosing a ring that not only looks the way you want it to, but also fits with your lifestyle. If you are someone who is very active, you may need to choose something more durable to suit your everyday activities. For example, if you rock climb or play any sports, you may want to consider a ring that can withstand such activities.

✦ QUICK TIPS FOR RING SHOPPING ✦

- Stay within your budget. While a ring is important, it's the marriage that counts.

- Opt for a ring that feels comfortable on your finger. You don't want to wear something that hurts your finger or is too tight or too big. Work with your jeweler to ensure it fits well.

- Choose a ring you can wear with your other everyday jewelry. Try to be as realistic as possible with the style of wedding ring you will wear every day. You don't want to pick silver if your usual go-to is gold.

- Durability is key. While remaining in your budget, choose something that you trust will stand the test of time. Yes, the look is important, but you want durability to be at the top of your priority list, too.

—» ask mariah «—
Your Ring Questions

Who should be in charge of our rings on our wedding day?

The main goal, of course, is to have the rings land safely in both of your hands by the time you are at the altar or about ready to say "I do." Coming from the perspective of tradition, the best man would be responsible for holding on to the rings throughout the day and ensuring that they make it safely to the wedding ceremony. If there will be a ring bearer, they would be the one to walk the rings down the aisle and carefully hand them back to the best man, who would have given them to the ring bearer in the first place.

You can stick to tradition or you can choose whoever you trust most to hold on to the rings. Another variation you may see or be interested in implementing at your own wedding is for the ring bearer to hand the rings directly to the officiant.

In the case of a couple using a wedding planner, the wedding planner may hold on to the rings until the ceremony as well. The "how" in this situation is certainly less important than the "what." Your only goal is to give the ring to someone you trust wholeheartedly, who will ensure they make it into your hands when you find yourself ready to say "I do."

Should my wedding ring match my engagement ring?

There is no rule that says it should! This decision is completely based on your personal preference and what works best for your personal style. You may choose to get rings that complement each other as a couple, or perhaps you have two completely different styles! It also depends on how you plan to wear your rings or bands.

Traditionally, people choose to wear their engagement ring and wedding ring/band on the same finger: the left ring finger. In this scenario, the engagement ring would sit above the wedding ring/band. If this is what you choose to do, then you may want to consider using a similar style to your engagement ring.

Is there a difference between a wedding band and a wedding ring?

A wedding ring typically contains diamonds or other stones, whereas a wedding band is a solid piece of metal without stones. What you choose for your wedding is entirely up to you.

What are some ways we can make our wedding bands unique?

The style of your wedding bands will be completely up to you and your fiancé. Like everything else in the wedding planning process, shopping for rings will require a bit of pre-work and discussion. Take some time to research different options together. Similarly to how you may have created a vision board for your dress, you might want to consider doing the same for your rings.

Do you want your and your partner's rings to match? Some couples may opt for an engraving, a special stone gemstone, or finish to make their rings stand out. If you are working with a jeweler, communicate your desire for more personalized or unique wedding bands to them as they are truly the experts in this situation and may have some creative ideas to share with you.

In essence, you want something you and your partner will be happy with.

Bridal Shower, Wedding Shower & Bach Parties

There are a few key events in a traditional wedding process that might occur during your wedding planning that also require their own preparation. Let's begin with the bridal or wedding shower. The tradition of a bridal shower stems back to the sixteenth century and has significantly evolved since then, as have many wedding traditions. The purpose of a bridal shower was to get the bridal party and close women wedding guests together to celebrate the bride and to "shower" her with gifts. Today you can take the traditional route or a more modern and less-traditional approach, which we will touch on in a bit. This is where your registry comes in, too.

Other traditions of the wedding process include the bachelorette and bachelor parties. These parties were created to be the last "hoorah" for the couple before it was time for them to get married. Historically, they would take place very close to the wedding day, if not the night before. Today, your bach parties can be whatever you want them to be. More on this a little later, but first, let's break down some of the components of a traditional bridal shower, and what your role is as the person getting married.

✤ Hosting a Bridal Shower ✤

Who is supposed to host the shower? Historically, this would fall under the responsibility of the maid or matron of honor. However, the financial responsibility of being a member of a wedding party has drastically changed since these traditions came to be. Today we see any close family member or friend, or a group of them together, hosting the shower in conjunction with the person of honor.

Another past tradition was to surprise the bride and not have her involved in any of the planning. Now we see more and more couples playing an active role in the planning process of their shower.

If you want to take a more modern approach to a bridal shower, a less-traditional option that has become more common in our present day is having a wedding shower in place of a bridal shower.

✤ Bridal Shower vs. Wedding Shower ✤

What is the difference between a bridal and a wedding shower? A wedding shower would be thrown for the couple instead of the bride only, and close family and friends along with the entire wedding party would be invited. In simple terms, it would be a co-ed celebration to "shower" the couple with gifts instead of just the bride. This may be something you throw for yourselves, or perhaps a family member or the wedding party would host for you. A bridal shower, as I mentioned earlier, is a celebration of the bride with her bridal party usually planned by the matron of honor.

In short, you can choose to take the traditional route and have a bridal shower, opt for something less-traditional like a joint wedding shower, or perhaps you and your partner decide not to have any type of shower at all. Don't feel obligated to do anything that doesn't feel like something you or your partner would want as a part of celebrating your marriage. Do what works best for you

❧ Thank-Yous for Your Shower ❧

As the bride or member of the couple, you have two main tasks to complete when it comes to your own bridal/wedding shower. The first is in how you thank your hosts, and the second is in how you thank your guests. You want to make sure you plan to give your hosts a small gift along with a handwritten note to thank them for hosting your shower. Some of my favorite gift ideas are candles, linen cocktail napkins, tea towels, or something personalized for their home. You can bring the gift for them to the shower or send it to them after the fact.

It would not be necessary to get your person of honor a gift for the shower specifically, as you may prefer to purchase a gift to thank them for all of their duties as a person of honor upon completion of all wedding festivities. If your person of honor is planning and paying for the entire shower, then you may decide to do otherwise.

Next, you will want to write thank-you notes to everyone who brought or sent a gift to your shower. This includes those who were unable to attend but sent a gift in their absence. There is a general etiquette guideline that dictates if you open a gift in front of the person who gave it to you, you do not have to send a thank-you note. However, this guideline does not apply to shower gifts. Thank-you cards should be sent out regardless of whether or not you chose to open your gifts at your shower. Please see the thank-you note chapter for specific etiquette.

·» Bach Parties «·

In a traditional marriage, the groom's close male friends and family members would take him out for an evening of fun, and the same would happen for the bride and her female friends and family. A single-evening bash quickly evolved into elaborate long-weekend trips that typically occur anywhere from two to three months prior to the wedding.

In today's world, your bach parties can be as elaborate or as simple as you desire—and as your budget allows. You can make your bach celebration a trip, a party, a day event, or even have a double bach for you and your significant other.

Social media seems to constantly remind us of how expensive and detail-oriented these trips can be. Despite what your budget is, there are still ways you can make the festivities extra special. You may want to consider certain decorations, small gifts for your wedding party that may be something they can use or wear on the trip, a series of games, and a special noteworthy activity that becomes the highlight of the trip.

And remember, if you prefer not to have a celebration like this for whatever reason, that is completely up to you! Now, if you are still interested in celebrating, but your budget doesn't allow for such an elaborate celebration, there are other ways to celebrate with your closest friends and family members. You can host a cooking experience, karaoke night, or a game night at home. You can have a virtual party where you gather your closest friends and play games. Or consider a low-key outdoor celebration such as a picnic or beach day.

TIP ❥ *Be sure to discuss with your partner whether or not you are both comfortable having a bach party or festivities and what the boundaries are for these events.*

ask mariah
Your Shower & Bach Party Questions

How do I ask someone to host a shower for me?

Let this responsibility fall on your person of honor. Have a discussion with your person of honor to determine who they could potentially ask to help them host and plan the shower—they may want to join forces with your closest family members to come up with a plan. With that being said, there is a chance a family member or friend may just step forward and offer to host. If you want to go the old-school way and be surprised, it will be up to your person of honor to arrange the details.

Who should be invited to our shower?

When referring to a traditional wedding, the bridal party as well as any close women guests are typically invited to join in on the festivities. For couples wanting to take a more modern approach to a shower, close friends, family members, and the wedding party would be included. However, anyone who is invited to the shower should also have received a "save-the-date" or invitation for your wedding depending on the timing of the shower. You do not need to invite people who are attending your wedding as a partner or plus-one of a guest you have a close relationship with. If you are involved in the planning process, it may be helpful to work with your hosts and provide some insight as to whom you would like to see invited to your shower.

What if my friends at work want to throw me a shower but they are not invited to my wedding?

There is no exact time for when the shower should happen, but somewhere between two and four months before the wedding day is standard. If you as the bride or person getting married are not directly involved in the planning process, you may not have control over when it happens. Additionally, it's gracious to be flexible toward your hosts' schedules and plans.

When should the shower take place?

There is no exact time for when the shower should happen, but somewhere between two and four months before the wedding day is standard. If you as the bride or person getting married are not directly involved in the planning process, you may not have control over when it happens. Additionally, it's gracious to be flexible toward your hosts' schedules and plans.

What should be included on a shower invitation?

Bridal or wedding shower invitations should be sent out at least six weeks prior to the shower date. Your shower invitation will be less elaborate than your wedding invitation bundle. Again, you may not be involved in the planning, but if you are, you can choose to use the invitation designer you have been using, or you can let your hosts take care of it. The invitations should be sent by your hosts, and they should also be handling the RSVP details. A proper shower invitation should contain the following things:

- A heading/introduction indicating that the guest has been invited to celebrate the bride-to-be or couple-to-be at their bridal or wedding shower.

- When the event is taking place.

- Where the event is taking place.

- A request for a response.

- Registry information, a separate registry card, or wedding website URL. (Note: There should be one registry only for your entire wedding.)

You may be thinking, "Didn't I read somewhere in this book that registry information should not be included on invitations?" You are not wrong! It is a faux pas to include specific registry information on your wedding invitation, but it is perfectly acceptable and encouraged to include the necessary information on the shower invitation.

What should take place at a bridal shower?

Bridal showers come in many shapes and sizes and can be anything from a backyard gathering, all the way to a formal luncheon, afternoon tea at a venue, and everything in between. There is often time set aside to play games or get everyone together in a special way to honor the bride. It is traditional for brides to open their gifts in front of their guests, too. Unlike the actual wedding, it is both encouraged and usual for guests to bring physical gifts to the shower unless differently stated on the registry.

Some guests will choose to purchase gifts from the registry whereas others will choose to shop for their own gift for you or you and your partner. This poses the question: "What if I don't want to open my gifts in front of everyone?" If opening your gifts is something the host intentionally planned for, it would be in your best interests to respect their plan and the work they put into setting up this shower. However, if you feel strongly about not doing this, simply let your person of honor or host know ahead of time. Just prepare accordingly for the strong likelihood of an older guest approaching you and asking why you are not opening gifts!

TIP ➤ *If you do choose to open gifts in front of everyone, designate someone in your bridal party to write down who gave you what. This will come in handy later when it's time to write thank-you notes.*

How do you kindly let your host(s) know what you want your shower to be/look like?

Your host has so graciously offered to plan and pay for a party that is all about you, so it would be in poor taste to then tell the hosts how they should plan your shower. While their style may differ from yours, you want to accept this kind gesture with grace and gratitude. With that said, if you are involved in the planning process in any way, you're allowed to want your shower to be something you've envisioned, one that feels and looks like you, and one that matches the overall branding and formality of your entire wedding.

TIP > *Let this fall completely on your person of honor. A specific request will sound entirely better coming from her than it would coming from you. Your person of honor is most likely a best friend, sister, or family member, so you should be able to talk candidly with them about what your heart desires. Then you leave it up to them to convey any specific wishes in a tasteful manner.*

Who is supposed to plan the bach festivities?

The persons of honor would spearhead the planning for bach parties. Similar to the bridal/wedding shower, as the person getting married, you can be as involved as you would like to be in the planning process. Some couples prefer to plan their parties alongside their person of honor, and some prefer to be left out of the planning process for more of a surprise factor. While the person of honor would be the commander of the plans, it is very common for the other attendees to also be involved and help with the planning process.

Who goes on the trip or joins for the night out?

If you have a wedding party, they are all typically included. If there are any close friends or family members who were not part of the wedding party for whatever reason, they also may join in on the festivities. If you do not have a wedding party, the invitees would be a small group of people closest to you.

What are the financial responsibilities involved in a bach trip?

Although the person of honor would be in charge of the planning process, they are not hosting it. This is important to remember because a host would be responsible for paying for an event in addition to planning it, as we discussed earlier on page 130. Because your person of honor would not be playing the role of the host, everyone is responsible for paying their own way. Depending on each group's situation and preference, they may also pay for some of your trip expenses as well. This is exactly why it is so crucial to be up front with your wedding party about the expected financial responsibilities, as we discussed on pages 60 to 61. When you ask your wedding party to be a part of your special day, you most likely will not know exactly how much a bach trip might cost; however, you can plan for a general number so there are no surprises when it comes time to plan the trip. Communicating this budget to the person planning the trip will help ensure everyone is on the same page regardless of how involved you are in the planning process.

TIP ❯ *If you are looking to take a more modern approach to the traditional bach activities, consider a joint party or trip as a couple with your entire wedding party.*

My partner wants me to invite one of their family members to my party, but I don't want them to come. How can I handle this without offending my partner?

You may consider reserving your bach party for your wedding party only. This way, you are not offending anyone else. If you are not having a wedding party or this person is part of your wedding party, have an open and honest conversation with your partner about how you feel about the situation.

Beauty Routine & Poise for Events

It's safe to say that looking and feeling your best on your wedding day is an absolute necessity. In this chapter, I am going to walk you through some of my tips and tricks to help you shine. We will discuss some things you can do leading up to each event, as well as things you can do at these events to present yourself in the best and most poised way possible.

There seems to be more and more pressure being put on people who are getting married when it comes to their self-care and preparation regimen for their wedding day. Not to mention, this preparation comes with a big time commitment and an even bigger price tag. My only goal is to give you tools to enhance the best version of yourself. The tips and tricks included in this chapter may be new things you will decide to implement specifically for your special wedding season, or they may be things you already do, and it's just about taking them to the next level.

❧ Preparation and Routine ❧

The first step in your beauty and wellness preparation journey is to make the commitment to yourself about six months before your wedding. At this beginning point, I also recommend consulting with any professionals you will be working with to come up with your plan and recommended timing for the below steps.

✦ BEGIN A MINDFULNESS PRACTICE ✦

Beauty will always come from within. If you want to shine on your special day, you have to start on the inside, and a great way to do this is through an intentional mindfulness practice. Whether this be meditation, affirmations, journaling, a creative hobby, or anything that may work best for you, you want to make sure you are in the right mindset. Within this mindfulness practice, it's essential that the voice inside of your head is speaking kindly toward you, too.

✦ OPT FOR A HEALTHY DIET FOR YOUR BODY ✦

The real secret to a glowing complexion also starts from within. You can have a top-notch, consistent skin care regimen leading up to your wedding, which is important too, but the real trick is to be mindful of what you are consuming. This will not only make you look your best, but it will also help you feel your best. Being consistent with healthy eating choices that work well for your body is sure to help you radiate from within on your wedding day. You can consult a dietician, nutritionist, or doctor to help find what is best for you and your health.

✦ DRINK PLENTY OF WATER ✦

Get in the habit of drinking lots of water as soon as you can. This is another secret to glowing skin!

✦ EXERCISE ✦

Find a form of movement that you truly enjoy and look forward to doing daily. Not only will this help you look and feel your very best, but it's also an excellent form of stress relief.

✦ STEP UP YOUR ORAL-HYGIENE GAME ✦

A beautiful and healthy smile is a must. Be sure to make an appointment to see your dentist to go over any special care plans that you may be interested in pursuing leading up to your wedding, such as teeth whitening.

✦ KEEP YOUR IMMUNE SYSTEM IN TIP-TOP SHAPE ✦

While eating healthy, exercising, and drinking plenty of water will support your immune system naturally, you will want to take it even a step further during this time. Consult your doctor about a vitamin and supplement regimen to ensure you are supporting yourself in the necessary ways during a high-stress and exciting time in your life.

FIND A GOOD SKIN CARE ROUTINE
✦ AND BE CONSISTENT! ✦

This may be a place where you'll want to consult an expert, whether it be a licensed esthetician, dermatologist, or skin care salesperson/educator to see what your skin needs at that six-month mark, and in the lead-up to your wedding. They will be able to help you choose what products are best so you are spending your money wisely. Once you have a skin care routine that works really well, it's all about consistency, and pairing it with the other steps on this list.

✦ DO HAIR AND MAKEUP TRIALS ✦

If you are having your hair and makeup professionally done, be sure to schedule a trial so there are no surprises on your wedding day. If you are doing your own hair and makeup, or having a friend or family member do it, you should still consider having a practice run. During your trials, consult with the experts to see if there is anything you should be doing to prepare within that six-month period.

If you are thinking about changing anything about your hair before the wedding, such as style or color, you will want to test that out six months in advance too, to make sure your vision comes to life correctly, and so there is plenty of time for any damage control.

You can also use this time for educational purposes, especially if you will be doing your own hair and makeup for any wedding-related events. For instance, you can go visit a beauty supply store and speak with an employee who will help you choose the products that will work best for your skin and hair.

✦ TAKE CARE OF THOSE EYEBROWS ✦

Having your eyebrows properly groomed and shaped will be a game changer for your overall appearance. It is one of the best ways to enhance your natural beauty, give your face dimension, and flatter your features. This is one of the points where I strongly recommend you consult an expert. Begin six months out to create your growth and styling plan, and be consistent with appointments up until your wedding day.

ADD REGULAR MANICURES AND PEDICURES
❖ TO YOUR ROUTINE ❖

You may be someone who already does this. Whether it be a DIY mani-pedi or a trip to the salon, incorporating intentional nail care to your routine ahead of time will ensure your nails are healthy and strong for each wedding event. Additionally, it will give you plenty of time to test out different shapes, colors, and technicians (if you choose to use one) so you are perfectly pleased by your wedding day.

CONSIDER TREATING YOURSELF TO SPECIAL BEAUTY
❖ TREATMENTS WITHIN YOUR BUDGET ❖

What better time to give yourself a little extra pampering than in the months leading up to one of the most important and exciting days of your life? There are plenty of special treatments and care that you can treat yourself with depending on your budget, such as facials, laser hair removal, hair gloss treatments, eyebrow microblading, at-home spa days, etc.

MAKE SURE YOU ARE TAKING THE TIME
❖ TO REST AND SLEEP ❖

Extra rest will be so important not only for your physical health, but also to keep you focused and grounded so you can make all of these big decisions and even have some potentially tricky conversations that may come with wedding planning.

TIP ❯ *Make all of your appointments in advance for each special event and your actual wedding day. These appointments can include, but are not limited to, haircuts, hair color touch-up, mani-pedis, tanning, eyebrow waxing, facials, etc. This will keep you organized and ensure you can get an appointment with your desired technician at your preferred time.*

⇝ Poise for Each Event ⇜

Now that we've covered the preparation part of things, let's discuss a few key points for a polished and poised appearance for each of your special events.

EAT AND DRINK PLENTY OF WATER
✦ THE DAY OF EACH EVENT ✦

While this one may seem obvious, it's easy to get caught up in the excitement and nerves of these big days. There are so many things you want to make sure go right that you may find you end up putting yourself last! It is so important to eat regularly and drink plenty of water, regardless of how busy or nervous you may be, to give yourself the fuel you need to show up with poise at your special events.

✦ WORK ON POSTURE AND BODY LANGUAGE ✦

I had to squeeze "shoulders back!" in here somehow—it is an etiquette book, after all! Not only is good posture and positive body language an automatic way to make you look more polished, but it's also a major confidence booster. And as a bonus, you will look extra graceful in all of your photos.

✦ REFRESH YOUR DINING ETIQUETTE ✦

I recommend taking a mini dining etiquette refresher through a course or credible research. All eyes will be on you, even when you are enjoying an hors d'oeuvre or sipping on champagne. Being prepared will make you feel confident and at ease to move about each event with poise.

✦ TAKE THE TIME TO THANK EVERYONE ✦

Nothing is more graceful and polished than being well-spoken and displaying gratitude. It is imperative that you carve out the time to thank your guests, and enuinely show how much it means to you that they have decided to celebrate ith you. We will discuss this further in the reception chapter.

✧ TAKE TIME TO DE-STRESS ✧

our energy will show! Make sure you are taking the time to do the things you eed to do so that you are in the best mental state you can be in, and so you re able to show up for your partner and loved ones.

hink about the things that you do that help keep you calm and try to do some f those things at the beginning of your day before you go into go-mode. It's easy) get caught up planning everything and trying to get everything just right that ou forget to take a breath and take it all in. De-stressing will help you stay calm nd keep the people around you calm, too. Calm minds equal clear heads.

✧ THINGS TO HELP YOU DE-STRESS ✧

lere are some suggestions of things you can do to de-stress. It can sometimes e the simple things that help keep you levelheaded.

- Take a deep breath
- Take a walk outside or breathe in some fresh air
- Listen to your favorite music or song
- Take a quick nap
- Get your favorite food, snack, or drink
- Check in with yourself and take the time to write your feelings in a journal
- Meditate
- Dance!
- Watch your favorite show
- Talk to your loved ones

— ask mariah —
Your Beauty Routine Questions

I have turned into a bridezilla. How can I redeem myself?

Planning a wedding can be intense, emotional, and demanding. It can also be magical, exciting, and special. If it seems like the stressors have gotten the best of you, there are absolutely ways you can come back from that. First of al make sure you are taking care of your mental and physical health throughout the whole process. It is important to be aware of your limitations and capacity and to know when it is time to take a break or ask for help.

If you've found yourself lashing out at a family member, vendor, your person of honor, or even your partner, communication is key. A simple apology and heartfelt conversation will usually do the trick. If it seems the issue requires something greater than a conversation, you can always send a handwritten note and some flowers. The people closest to you will know that this is a stressful yet exciting time for you. Don't make them your punching bag!

What if my significant other has become a bridezilla? How can I approach them and not hurt their feelings?

This is definitely a delicate situation as you want to approach your partner while also being considerate of what they may be feeling during this time. Planning a wedding and other events relating to a wedding can certainly be stressful, especially the closer you get to these wedding events happening. Most likely, your significant other may be feeling overwhelmed with all the planning. While that is not an excuse for their behavior, you should take a gentle approach when talking with your partner about their behavior. You cannot control how they react, but you can certainly control how you approach them.

While individual situations will differ, and it truly depends on what is going on with your partner and your relationship, keep an open mind and heart, remember why you fell in love with your partner, and ask them how you can help. Step in when needed and try to give your partner space to take time to de-stress. Perhaps surprise your partner with some much-needed de-stressing time, such as taking them out to eat their favorite food, giving them a spa day, or simply carrying out smaller tasks throughout the day so they can take a break.

If I am having a destination wedding, how can I ensure my makeup artist and hairstylist can work with my hairstyle or skin type/tone?

Do your research before going to your destination, even if you are getting married in a resort that supplies a hairstylist and/or makeup artist. When looking into hairstylists and/or makeup artists, there is nothing wrong with asking if they have had experience working with your hair and skin type. It is better to inquire about this outright rather than assume or take any chances.

It will also be important to read reviews as well as look through social media or website photographs to make yourself familiar with their work. While it is best to schedule trials, you may not have the luxury of doing so with a destination wedding. This is why reviews, photographs, and personal recommendations will be crucial.

If I do not have the budget to make appointments for hair, makeup, etc., to prepare myself and/or vet the vendors for my big day, what is the next best thing to do?

There are plenty of things you can do that will come with a smaller price tag! For starters, if an entire appointment is not in the budget, visit a beauty supply store and lean on their expert staff members to show you a few special products that may help get your hair and skin ready. Additionally, there are thousands of online resources out there that share wonderful DIY things that you can make and do from the comfort of your own home with products that you may already have in your kitchen. Also, you can enlist any friends or family members for help with DIY things.

The Wedding

It's the moment you've all been waiting for . . . it's time to talk about the actual wedding! We have spent so much time assembling the base and filling in the details to help us get to the place of structuring the big events. We are going to cover each wedding event flow and logistics in detail, including any preparation that is still left for you to consider. By the end of this section, you will feel completely confident in detailing everything from your rehearsal dinner to the reception, and even what comes after.

We will cover everything from who gives speeches and when, to how to conduct your ceremony based on where it is taking place, to who walks down the aisle when, to how to organize your reception. There are also details included regarding other events you may be having, such as a bridal luncheon or welcome party. You will also finish this section having all the etiquette information you need as pertains to gifts and thank-you notes. Everything we have covered thus far has led us to this point, so without further ado . . .

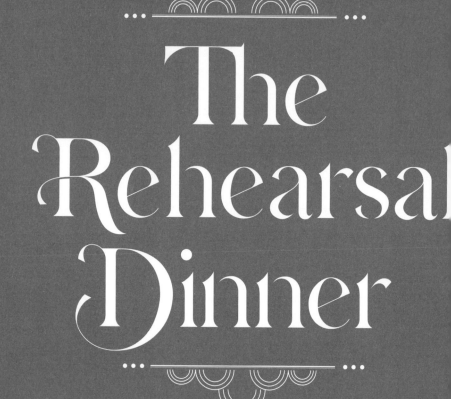

The
Rehearsal
Dinner

The purpose of a rehearsal dinner is exactly as it states: to rehearse! Traditionally, the rehearsal dinner takes place on the evening before the wedding day, allows everyone involved in the ceremony to learn the ceremony logistics and practice them, and is typically followed by a sit-down dinner.

Some dinners will include a small cocktail hour, while some will simply be a dinner only. A couple may opt to have their rehearsal dinner on their wedding venue property, if that is applicable, or somewhere nearby. It is rarer to see them held in a private home, although there is no rule that states otherwise. Some couples may decide to have a welcome party after rehearsing in place of a dinner, especially if they are having a destination wedding. We will discuss welcome parties in more detail on page 179.

❖ Planning a Rehearsal Dinner ❖

Your rehearsal dinner can truly be as casual and intimate or elaborate and formal as you want it to be. If you are having a themed wedding, this will be a good opportunity for you to keep up with that theme at your rehearsal dinner.

Here are some things you will want to consider when planning a rehearsal dinner:

- Who is hosting?
- Guest list (Remember, anyone you invite to your rehearsal dinner should also be invited to your wedding.)
- What will be served and how (e.g., open bar, family style, plated dinner, etc.)
- Any themes or decor you want to have
- Determining who, if anyone, will be giving toasts or speeches
- Communicating with your ceremony venue and/or officiant to plan for the actual rehearsing
- Communicating any last-minute reminders to your guests (e.g., wedding day schedule, dress codes, transportation details, etc.)

While traditional rehearsal celebrations occur over dinner, you may consider going a different route, such as planning a brunch or lunch. This may fit better within your budget, too, depending on who is hosting. Some couples will choose not to have a rehearsal celebration at all, but I would recommend to at least set time aside to rehearse with your wedding party and/or with your wedding officiant to ensure your ceremony runs as smoothly as possible.

⸭ Toasts and Speeches ⸭

It is both common and traditional to have toasts and speeches take place at a rehearsal dinner. The rehearsal dinner will most likely be a room filled with your closest friends and family members, so it is an intimate setting to take advantage of for this purpose. Many of the couple's loved ones will take this opportunity to tell personal stories in a less formal manner than would be expected at the wedding reception. A welcome toast would be given at the beginning of the meal by the host(s). A toast is not a speech, so this would only consist of a few sentences to welcome the guests and toast the future married couple. From there, the host can open the floor to the other guests, or you can choose to wait until the main course to begin the rest of the speeches.

TIP ≻ *Plan in advance whom you would like to give the speeches and toasts so that everyone understands the expectations and timing. Choose someone in your wedding party or family to help take charge of the speeches in terms of calling up the next guest and closing out the groups of speeches.*

Because the rehearsal dinner is a less formal and more intimate event, unplanned speeches may be given by friends and family members who feel called to say a few words. Your people of honor typically speak at the wedding reception, so you may want to use this opportunity to give others the chance to speak. Don't stress if the toasts and speeches don't go perfectly to plan. The rehearsal dinner is a really special opportunity to bring your closest loved ones together in a place you can really be present in. Soak up the love!

As with other wedding traditions, this is one you can take or leave. You may prefer to keep it more low-key and not have any toasts or speeches during your rehearsal dinner. However, I would recommend that both you and your host(s) (if you and your partner are not hosting) at least thank your guests for joining you in this special celebration.

–» *ask mariah* «–
Your Rehearsal Dinner Questions

Who is supposed to host the rehearsal dinner?

Speaking from a traditional place, the rehearsal dinner would be hosted by the groom's family under the assumption that the bride's family would be hosting the actual wedding. Today, anyone can host the rehearsal dinner, but it will typically remain contingent on who is hosting the wedding. If both partners' families are contributing to the wedding, both families may host the rehearsal dinner together. If the couple themselves is hosting the wedding, they may also host the rehearsal dinner, or perhaps a family member or friend would offer to do so.

The rehearsal dinner is a separate event from the wedding, regardless of who hosts, so a separate invitation is typically sent out to the guests who are invited. Similar to all of the invitations we've covered so far, this would be sent out by the host, who would also handle the RSVP process. The invitation would be simple and include a pre-addressed and postage-return envelope for responses.

Do we have to create and send invitations for our rehearsal dinner?

The short answer is no. It is not a requirement for you to create a separate formal invitation for the rehearsal dinner; however, if you want to create a virtual invitation or something less formal to let guests know when and where the rehearsal dinner will take place, you can certainly do that. You can also add rehearsal dinner information to your wedding website.

Who should be invited to the rehearsal dinner?

This is very much up to the hosts and the couple—but let's talk about the "musts." All immediate family (on both sides!) and the wedding party are typically included. This is because these are the groups of people who will likely be involved in your ceremony processional, and you need them to be present in order to rehearse. Some couples will consider inviting extended family from out of town who arrive early. Beyond that, you don't want your rehearsal dinner to turn into a mini-wedding, so you may want to communicate to your host that you want to keep it small.

Do we actually need to rehearse at the rehearsal dinner?

In the essence of good etiquette, you don't want to keep your guests waiting at your ceremony on the day of. Plus, there will be so much excitement and so many distractions that there will not be time or room for any practice come the big day. It is in your best interest to, at the least, discuss the logistics of the ceremony so everyone involved knows what to expect. You may be having your rehearsal dinner at a completely different location than your wedding ceremony, so you may have to use your imagination when it comes to practicing. Preparation equals poise!

Should we create a seating chart for our rehearsal dinner?

This will depend on the formality of your event and who is hosting this event. Typically, rehearsal dinners tend to be less formal than weddings and wouldn't really require a seating chart unless you want to include one or are having a very formal rehearsal dinner. Or if you have certain people that really can't be seated together then perhaps a seating chart would be helpful. Otherwise, seating charts are not mandatory for this type of event.

The Ceremony

Now, on to the part where you actually get to say "I do!"—the ceremony. While the goal and result will pretty much be the same across the board, each couple's ceremony is likely to look at least a little bit different. When you take into consideration various cultural and religious traditions as well as personal preferences, there are many different variations of a marriage ceremony.

The first thing you'll need to consider is whether you are getting married in a house of worship or at a neutral venue (either where your reception is, or a different one). It is more than likely that you decided on this in the early stages of your planning process. The reason this is so important to touch upon from an etiquette perspective is that religious ceremonies will often have requirements and certain protocols that you are expected to follow out of respect for the house of worship. This can range from the type of music that is allowed, to the order of the processional, all the way to certain religious requirements you need to obtain or complete in order to get married at that sacred venue. It is in your best interest to meet with the head of the house of worship or your religious officiant to ensure you are following the necessary steps to show the proper respect and have a successful and seamless ceremony experience.

❧ Ceremony Processional Order ❧

When it comes to getting married in a house of worship, the order of procession will most likely be an important aspect for you to follow and respect. Different religions have different orders, so it is best for you to work with your officiant to determine an order that works for your wedding style while simultaneously respecting the venue's protocol.

At a neutral venue, or non-religious ceremony, there is no true, correct order for a processional. It will depend on how many people/family members you want to have walk down the aisle. Here are three different examples of a potential processional order for a non-religious wedding that will respect an aspect of tradition, but also represent a modern approach.

TIP ❯ *It's important to find a wedding officiant who respects and honors your relationship. Don't be afraid to ask your officiant if they have experience officiating a wedding similar to yours before deciding to move forward with booking them.*

❖ PROCESSIONAL ORDER EXAMPLE 1 ❖

- Grandparents and extended family
- Groom's parents (or separately or just father)
- Mother of the bride (unless both parents are walking her down the aisle)
- Priest
- Groom (or groom with mother)
- Best man and maid of honor (can walk together or alone)
- Bridesmaids and groomsmen
- Ring bearer
- Flower girl
- Bride with father of the bride (or both parents)

✦ PROCESSIONAL ORDER EXAMPLE 2 ✦

- Officiant
- Partner 1 with parents
  (in a traditional wedding, this
  would typically be the groom)
- Wedding party

- Ring bearer
- Flower girl
- Partner 2 with parents
  (in a traditional wedding, this
  would typically be the bride)

✦ PROCESSIONAL ORDER EXAMPLE 3 ✦

- Officiant
- Partner 1's parents
- Partner 2's parents

- Wedding party
- Partner 1 (alone)
- Partner 2 (alone)

⋇ Exchanging Vows ⋇

Another aspect of the ceremony that you will have to consider is how the vows are exchanged. In a house of worship, there may be a very specific way in which this is done, and there may be a rule or tradition in place that the officiant reads certain vows. If you are having a non-religious ceremony, you will want to consider how you exchange your vows. Will you have your officiant read vows that you've written? Will they read generic vows? Will you read your own vows? Will you have a mix of religious or traditional vows and your own vows? The method of exchanging vows will certainly depend on your venue, religion, and/or personal preferences as a couple.

✻ Seating Guests ✻

Your guests will, of course, be an integral part of your ceremony as well. In a traditional wedding, family, friends, and guests of the bride would sit on the left side of the aisle, and the groom's guests would sit on the right side (facing the front). The reason why is because those are the sides the bride and groom would stand on with their accompanying wedding party members. Many couples take a more modern approach to this tradition by encouraging their guests to sit wherever they are most comfortable. Oftentimes, there is even signage located at the entrance of the ceremony that suggests where guests can sit.

No matter how you and your partner choose to stand at the front of the ceremony, or how you choose to seat your guests, there is one more thing you may want to consider when it comes to your ceremony seating, and that is reserving seats for family.

As a wedding guest, it is most appropriate to avoid sitting in the first few rows under the assumption that immediate family will sit there. However, not all guests get this hint. For this reason, you may want to consider finding a creative way to reserve a few seats for your immediate family. You can do this tastefully by adding a beautiful bow, flower petals, or another aspect of your ceremony decor to make these seats stand out. Plus, it is a nice way to give special attention to family members who may not be included in the procession.

–» ask mariah «–
Your Ceremony Questions

My family is religious and expects me to get married in our religion's house of worship. However, my partner and I prefer to get married at the venue where our reception is taking place. How do I make sure I am honoring my family's tradition while still having the ceremony we want?

The simple answer here is to incorporate as much tradition as you can into your ceremony, no matter where it is taking place. See where you can add elements to your decor, your vows, and the actual steps of your ceremony, and even consider ways you can get your family involved to celebrate and honor the religion.

We are an interfaith couple and both of our families want us to get married in their respective houses of worship. How do we compromise and honor both of our religions at our ceremony?

You have two roads you can take in this situation in order to make this compromise successful. The first is to have your ceremony in a neutral location and have two officiants who will work together to ensure both religions are being honored. Choosing a neutral location will ensure you, as a couple, are not favoring one tradition over another. The second road you can take is to have two different ceremonies, if that is important to you both. You will have to factor in extra planning, logistics, and, of course, money, but if it is nonnegotiable for you, your partner, and your families, it is certainly doable.

We are an LGBTQ+ couple. How do you recommend we approach walking down the aisle?

One option you may want to consider is walking with your parents or family members one after another. A modern approach would be to consider walking down the aisle together at the end of the processional. If you are not getting married in a house of worship where you have to honor certain traditions and protocols, it is truly up to you how you decide to conduct the processional! Lean on your officiant for assistance and suggestions, too.

The processional may be the first time we are seeing each other as a couple. So, to have a "first look" or to not have a "first look"?

A "first look" is when the couple sees each other in an intimate moment before the ceremony. It usually takes place with just the two of them plus a photographer and/ or videographer. Many couples will choose to do a "first look" so they can take photos before the ceremony, freeing up their time between the ceremony and reception. It also poses as a wonderful photo opportunity. The downside to a "first look" that couples will consider is the element of surprise it takes away when the couple walks down the aisle for the first time. There is no right or wrong answer as this is completely a personal preference. You will have to consider the flow and timing of your wedding events, and how you want to see each other first.

How do we politely let our guests know that my partner and I have decided to have a phone-less ceremony?

There are three main ways that come to mind. The first is to note it on your website under the ceremony details, such as location, time, and dress code. The second is to have signage that matches your ceremony decor right outside of the entrance. The third is to have your officiant make an announcement at the beginning of the ceremony. You can choose one of these options or use all three

Is the ceremony an appropriate time to honor deceased loved ones?

Many couples will utilize the ceremony as an opportunity to honor deceased family members. What is the best way to approach this? If you are getting married in a house of worship, they may have a designated method of honoring deceased family members, perhaps through a particular prayer or ritual. Regardless of your ceremony venue, you may want to consider saving a seat dedicated to them, including a note in the wedding program if you choose to have one, having a moment of silence, having a small table with photos and candles, or having a member of your family or yourself say a few words in honor of them.

What happens after the ceremony is complete?

Well, if you asked this question several years ago, the answer would be the receiving line. A receiving line would typically occur immediately following the ceremony. The guests would form a line to speak to the newly married couple, which would give the couple a chance to display their gratitude to each guest, and it would give the guests the opportunity to personally congratulate the couple. The wedding hosts and wedding party would often stand next to the couple to assist with greeting guests. Are receiving lines a thing of the past? While they are certainly less common nowadays, they remain a good opportunity for you to thank your guests, which of course is so important. We will discuss another method on how to do this in the next chapter.

The
Reception

It's time to celebrate! In this chapter we will cover everything
you need to know about reception etiquette. This is where your creative
vision will really come to life! There certainly is not a one-size-fits-all
way to format a wedding reception, as each one is unique. There is
a traditional order in which things are done at a reception, but this is
by no means the rule of how things should be done. As it has occurred
throughout the book already, I will share the tradition, and then you
can interpret it in a way that works well for your wedding style and
aligns with your preferences.

Regardless of whether or not your reception is at the same venue
as your ceremony, a cocktail hour may precede the actual reception.
Its purpose is to give everyone (meaning staff, vendor team, guests,
and you as the couple) some breathing room and a snack before the
big celebration. Think of it as an elegant transition period. If your
ceremony was in fact the first time you saw each other as a couple
because you chose not to do a "first look," the photographer will most
likely utilize the designated cocktail hour time to take photos of the
couple, immediate family, and wedding party.

⊹ Cocktail Hour ⊹

Traditional cocktail hours will take place in a separate room or location within the main venue and drinks and light bites are usually served by serving staff or buffet style. The area is usually sprinkled with a few high-top tables and/or tables with chairs, but there are no formal seating arrangements as most guests will choose to stand. Cocktail hours typically do not exceed ninety minutes as you do not want your guests to feel like they are spending too much time lingering. Some couples will choose to have their reception cocktail-style. If this is the case, it would not be necessary to have an additional cocktail hour or gathering time before the reception.

A cocktail hour would be the perfect place to display a signature cocktail. Having a signature cocktail is a wonderful way to add a personal touch to your festivities and give your guests an inside look into your personality as a couple. It also gives couples the chance to add a piece of their branding to the reception through a fun play on words, and even certain signage. Some couples may choose to have one signature cocktail, or even two to represent each of them. Signature cocktails may be served during the reception as well.

TIP ❯ *Consider offering a signature mocktail for guests who can't or prefer not to drink alcohol.*

⊹ Reception Kickoff ⊹

The reception kickoff would immediately follow the cocktail hour. Following is a general example of how a traditional wedding reception may play out. Again, feel free to use this as a guide, but remember that these are not rules written in stone. Your venue, vendor team, and/or wedding planner will be there to guide you and help you plan out the schedule that works best for your individual wedding style—especially if it is less traditional.

TRADITIONAL WEDDING RECEPTION SCHEDULE EXAMPLE:

- Guests transition from cocktail hour location to reception location

- Newlyweds' entrance

- Newlyweds' first dance

- Other first dances (e.g., bride and father of the bride)

- Blessings, toasts, and speeches

- Meal

- Dancing time

- Bouquet and garter toss

- Cake cutting

- More dancing

- Farewell

TIP ❯ *If you are having live music or a DJ at your wedding, they will play a huge role in ensuring that the flow of your celebration goes correctly. They will often announce the different components as they are ready to happen. For this reason, give your DJ or musician/singer a copy of the reception schedule ahead of time.*

When your guests transition from the cocktail hour to the reception you will need to consider whether or not you want to have assigned seating. If you are having a traditional wedding reception with a sit-down dinner, it is most likely in your best interest to arrange seating ahead of time, allowing guests to pick up place cards on the way into the reception. This will add a sense of organization and flow to your event and allows you to be in control of who sits where. This comes in especially handy if there are guests at your wedding who do not know each other or do not get along.

❧ Seating Chart ❧

What should you consider when planning the seating chart for your guests? First off, you want to work with your venue and/or wedding planner to determine the layout of the room and table sizes. Make a diagram to match the layout and amount of seats at each table, so you can easily fill the seats with your guest list. You will want to seat yourselves first, followed by your wedding party, your immediate family, and then extended family, friends, and other guests. You want to take into consideration age groups, who you want near each other, the overall flow of the layout, and special things like making sure elderly guests are not too close to the music speaker! If you need help, utilize your immediate family and wedding party to help you decide who should sit where. They are likely to know your friends and family just as well as you do!

Upon making your seating chart, you need some way to notify your guests as to where they are sitting. For a traditional sit-down dinner where guests either select what they would be eating on the invitation or will be ordering at the table, you will want to assign exact seats. For a buffet-style or family-style dinner, you may consider just assigning tables and letting guests choose where they sit at that table.

There are many creative and decorative ways to display table seating arrangements at the entrance of your reception. The most traditional way is to have a place card with your guests' names and table number, then an additional place card at the table where their specific seat is. You can also have a seating chart sign where everyone glances to see which table they are seated at.

∗ Guest Book and Gift Placement ∗

There are two more things you might want to consider placing with or near the seating chart or place cards: somewhere to leave cards and a guest book. Every good wedding guest knows they should not be bringing physical gifts to a wedding reception. However, always plan for the unexpected! Designate a place near the entrance where guests can leave cards and gifts, and work with a venue staff member or a member of your wedding party to ensure the gifts end up in the right place at the end of the reception.

Additionally, you may consider having a guest book for guests to sign. There are many creative ways that couples display a guest book, whether it be the traditional signing book with photos of the couple throughout the pages or leaving a polaroid camera for guests to take photos of themselves to paste into a memory book. Putting all of these things in one location makes it easy for guests to access them and remember to take part in them.

∗ Toasts and Speeches ∗

Next, let's talk about toasts and speeches. Unlike the rehearsal dinner, the wedding reception toasts and speeches are a bit more structured. This is not the time for open mic night! However, if your wedding reception is smaller and less traditional, you can be more lenient about this.

A welcome toast is typically given by the wedding host. In a modern wedding, both sets of parents or guardians are likely to want to speak. Next would be your persons of honor, such as the maid of honor and best man, and if there is not a wedding party, it could be a sibling or best friend.

You want to give a heads-up to your family and friends making speeches for how long they should be—three minutes is a safe length. If you or your partner wants to say a few words, let that be the last speech or toast that occurs. In a traditional wedding, your guests will already have been sitting for the entrance and first dances and are probably eager to start dancing by now! Food may begin to be served at this point in the reception.

TIP ❯ *Dining etiquette reminder! Do not drink from your glass when you are being toasted as it is equivalent to clapping for yourself when receiving a round of applause. Simply raise the glass to acknowledge the toast.*

❖ Food ❖

Speaking of food, let's discuss details. The style of your meal will be a major component to the formality of your wedding. A very formal wedding typically coincides with a formal sit-down meal. A less-formal wedding may also have a sit-down meal, but a buffet or family-style dinner may also work in this case. You will want to arrange with your venue how food will be served, or in what order tables will be called to enjoy the buffet, so you do not have your guests in line for the buffet when speeches and toasts are being given.

If food is being provided by the venue or through a caterer, it is likely that you will meet with them as early as four months prior to your wedding to plan out a general menu. This is when you will determine things, such as how many courses are being served, the style of the dining, and whether your guests will choose their food selection on their RSVP card versus orders being taken at the wedding. As your wedding date gets closer, it is also likely that you will meet with your venue or caterer for an official tasting to finalize your food plans.

Whether you are working with a florist, venue, or event planner to make your centerpieces, or you are making them yourself, make sure they are not too tall or wide that they block your guests' views of each other or the dance floor.

Another thing you want to remember when it comes to food is making sure your tables are set properly. If you are working with a venue that offers linens and cutlery, it is likely you will work with them to pick out exactly what you want to use. Otherwise, you may be renting or providing the table-setting pieces. Utilize this factor to add a fun design element to your reception space that reflects the formality and style of your wedding. Remember, set your tables properly!

✤ Cutting the Cake ✤

Another common tradition is the cutting of the cake. This is the point in the reception where, traditionally speaking, a cake would be rolled out to the center of the dance floor, and all eyes would be on the couple as they cut the first slice. Then the cake is brought back into the kitchen or different area, sliced, and distributed to guests. The history and tradition of cutting the cake was to signal to guests that the festivities would soon be over. You can expect some guests to leave after the cake cutting.

If you are following this traditional schedule and providing transportation for your guests back to your booked accommodation, you may want to consider having the first bus or other method of transportation to leave momentarily after dessert is served. If you do not choose to have or cut a cake, dessert may be served shortly after the fun rituals and traditions are complete. There is typically time for more dancing and celebration after this ritual is over.

Receiving Lines and
✵ Other Traditions ✵

Let's revisit the topic of receiving lines for a moment. Why were receiving lines important? It has traditionally been a moment to give the couple a chance to speak to the guests and thank them for being present to celebrate their wedding. Taking the time to speak to your guests is extremely important and a gracious thing to do. An alternative to a receiving line is to visit guests at their table while they are eating their meal. While this approach forces you and your partner to eat fairly quickly, it is the perfect time to make sure you are visiting each table, meaning you are seeing each guest. You only need to spend a few minutes at each table and engage in a general conversation, so you are not having an intimate conversation with just one or two guests.

There are various traditions that typically occur throughout a wedding reception, such as a bouquet and garter toss. You may find yourself wanting to participate in these traditions—or you may not! If I haven't said it enough times already, it is your wedding, and as long as you are being respectful and gracious to your guests, the amount of tradition you want to include in your wedding is up to you. The wedding reception is a great time to add other traditions in place of or in addition to typical ones like the bouquet and garter toss. You may have a specific cultural or religious tradition that you want to see take place.

It is important to discuss your exit strategy prior to the start of the event. Seems like we're jumping ahead too quickly, doesn't it? We might be, but it could also be helpful depending on what exit strategy you choose. You may simply want to wait at your venue until the very end, exiting along with your guests. Other couples will have their guests gather in a line, or even with sparklers, to watch them exit from the venue and get into their chosen mode of transportation. Are you picturing the "just married" carriages in the fairy tales? Having a plan ahead of time will ensure you and your partner are on the same page.

–» ask mariah «–
Your Reception Questions

How do I politely indicate that a seat is for my guest's plus-one?

If your guests sent in their response with their plus-one's name, the answer is simple. If this is not the case, that's where it gets a bit more gray. Firstly, reach out to ask your guest for the name of the person they will bring. If they do not know in time, the most polite way to handle this situation would be to use your guest's name and then add the word "guest" right after it (e.g., Ms. Melanie Taylor's Guest).

I did not give my friend a plus-one to the wedding, but they brought one anyway. How do I handle this, especially with assigned seating?

To try to avoid this situation as much as possible, make sure you are reading through the response cards with a fine-tooth comb. It may have been an innocent oversight by your guest, in which case you can politely clear the air before the actual wedding. If that isn't the case, and someone shows up uninvited, I would ask the staff or the host to quickly set an extra seat at the table if you are able to catch it in time. Although it is terribly inconvenient and undeniably rude for your guest to have done this, it wouldn't necessarily be right to kick someone out of your wedding. This person probably had no idea they weren't actually invited and can you imagine how embarrassing that would be?!

We can't afford a sit-down dinner and an open bar. Which should we spend our money on?

This truly depends on the formality and style of your wedding, and what is most important to you as a couple. If you don't want to have to choose one or the other, consider going for a happy medium. You can price out a few different options to see what works best for you and your partner in terms of budget. For example, you can have a buffet dinner and choose two signature cocktails guests can pick from. If they want something else to drink, that would be on their terms. Another example would be to only have beer and wine to accompany a smaller dinner buffet. When in doubt, making sure your guests are fed should be the top priority.

How do we accommodate a guest who has a severe food allergy or food restriction?

It is a wonderful gesture to add a space on your response card or on your wedding website for a guest to indicate a food allergy. Please note, you only need to accommodate guests with true allergies and restrictions, not preferences. A nut allergy, celiac disease, or being a vegetarian are allergies and restrictions. Following a keto diet or not liking a certain vegetable is a preference. If someone makes you aware of a certain allergy or restriction, there are a few measures you can take depending on your wedding style to ensure they are safe. If you are having a served sit-down dinner with designated seating, let the venue staff know where that specific guest will be seated ahead of time. If you are having a buffet-style dinner, make sure you note on the food titles what each contains or whether they are free of a certain allergen or allergens.

How do we deal with a guest who is particularly talkative during the reception?

If you find yourself cornered by a certain guest, or there is someone who is dominating the table conversation when you visit, you have the easiest excuse to get yourself out of this, and that is simply that you want to make sure you get to see and thank each guest before dancing begins. From an etiquette perspective, you don't want to leave a guest standing by themselves, so consider introducing them to another guest they may not know to allow you to continue greeting and thanking other guests.

How do we teach our guests about cultural or religious traditions that we want to have at our wedding that they may not be aware of or understand?

This would be the perfect opportunity to take advantage of your wedding website. You can make a special tab or section for unique traditions or rituals hat may take place at your ceremony or reception. You can explain what occurs and the why behind each one, so your guests of a different religion or culture can better understand when it comes time for the ritual or tradition to take place. Understanding the conventions ahead of time allows your guests to celebrate with you in the moment!

Our families are bilingual and most of our guests may not understand the same language as the other half, so how do we ensure everyone in our wedding understands what is going on at all times?

You may want to consider hiring a translator to join you for all of the wedding festivities to ensure your guests are able to follow along and enjoy themselves in an environment that is as stress-free as possible! This is something to consider during your discussions about budget. Or the other option is to enlist family members who are able to translate during your wedding.

How do we handle a guest who is acting inappropriately at our wedding?

The last thing you want to worry about is a guest who has had too much to drink or is simply acting out of character. If it gets to the point where it is unsafe and distracting for them to remain at your wedding, default to a venue staff member to kindly ask them to leave and offer to call them a mode of transportation. If a staff member does not exist in the case of your specific wedding style, ask a member of your wedding party or a family member. It takes the personal and/or insulting aspect out of it by leaving it for someone other than you or your partner to handle.

Do we need to give out wedding favors?

You are absolutely not required to give out wedding favors, but you can if you'd like to, and if your budget allows. If you chose to have welcome bags at your hotels, that may count as your favor. You can also decide to make a DIY wedding favor. You want to have something personalized with your name and wedding date for guests to easily grab on the way out. There is no proper etiquette when it comes to wedding favors, and this is an old-time tradition you can take or leave.

Other Events

I may sound like a broken record at this point, as I continue to say that this is your wedding so you can follow the traditions to a tee, or you can pick and choose which events and traditions you want included in your special events and which you'd rather leave out. In this chapter, we will cover some other events that you may choose to have as a part of your wedding festivities.

In terms of proper etiquette, there is less emphasis on the "how" for each of these events, but they all have one thing in common—and that is to consider and provide for your guests in additional ways. Do not feel guilty whatsoever if these events don't work with your budget or simply don't interest you. I am providing alternatives to events that will deliver the same message to your guests in another way.

❧ Bridal Luncheon ❧

A bridal luncheon is an intimate opportunity for the bride to personally thank her bridesmaids for all of the time, money, and energy they have put into this commitment. It is often planned and hosted by the bride (and potentially her family), with some help from the maid of honor. The only attendees would be the bridal party and any additional women guests of honor, which are usually members of the bride's immediate family, such as her mom, sisters, grandmothers, and aunts.

The bridal luncheon would take place just a few days before the wedding, on the day of the rehearsal dinner, or even the morning of the wedding while everyone is getting ready. Traditionally, it was a formal luncheon that would consist of a beautifully set table and light bites. The luncheon style was most common, but some brides may choose to honor their bridesmaids in a different way, such as group manicures, afternoon tea, a dinner party, a pajama party, etc. In the wedding party chapter we discussed purchasing any items for your bridesmaids that you want them to wear on your wedding weekend, such as pajamas, slippers, jewelry, or lip gloss. Your bridal luncheon would be the perfect time to present your bridal party with these gifts.

TIP ❯ *Include a personal, heartfelt, handwritten thank-you note for each member of your bridal party. Although you may have thanked them several times throughout the planning process, shower, bachelorette party, etc., this is the best opportunity to truly seal your intention and message as your wedding quickly approaches.*

Of course, while traditionally a bridal luncheon is reserved for brides and their bridal party, you can totally customize this to your own wedding style. You may also find yourself uninterested in having a traditional bridal luncheon. A fun and unique alternative could be a small post-wedding celebration where you could relive the special memories of the wedding weekend or day together, and hand out your thank you notes or gifts.

·» Welcome Party «·

Couples who choose to have a destination wedding will oftentimes host a welcome party as a component of the weekend festivities. A welcome party is typically an "open-house"-style cocktail party that takes place on the night before the rehearsal dinner. Destination weddings usually require guests to arrive a day or a few days prior to the first event. When most guests have to travel far for a wedding, it is a nice event to offer as a way to kick off the wedding festivities and give them something to do in an unfamiliar place. There is no rule as to who will host the welcome party, but it is usually the host or whomever is hosting the rehearsal dinner, as this often gets looped in with the pre-wedding activities.

TIP ❯ *It would not be proper etiquette to limit who you are inviting to a welcome party, especially if you are having a destination wedding. The etiquette here is different from a rehearsal dinner as not all guests expect an invitation to a rehearsal dinner.*

A welcome party can be as formal or informal as you choose. You can notify guests about the welcome party via your wedding website, or you can include a formal invitation card with your wedding invitation bundle. Remember, a rehearsal dinner and a wedding reception are just around the corner, so consider that when you and your hosts are planning the formality of the welcome party.

A welcome party is by no means necessary, even for a destination wedding. It is all about considering your guests' comfort and needs more than having another event. If you are not interested in having a welcome party, or your budget does not allow for one, there are plenty of things you can do to honor the fact that your guests are coming from out of town. You can list restaurants, sights, activities, and personal favorite spots on your wedding website and/or in your welcome letter. It will show your guests that you went through the effort of putting something together with the intention of making sure they are taken care of. Etiquette will always be about the message and intent behind something rather than the nitty-gritty details.

✺ The Morning-After Brunch ✺

Another wedding event you may have heard of, attended, or are interested in including in your weekend is a brunch the morning after the reception. This type of event is seen for both destination and local weddings. Some couples will have this brunch at the hotel or other accommodation where their guests are staying for the wedding weekend. It acts as a send-off so your guests can enjoy breakfast, recap the evening, and check out from the hotel. Some brunches are hosted at a small venue or family home if it is a local wedding, and may only be open to the wedding party and close family. (Think rehearsal dinner list.)

In a traditional situation where the bride's family would pay for the wedding, the groom's family would most likely host the brunch in addition to the rehearsal dinner. In modern times, you can follow this same format where whomever hosts the rehearsal dinner would also host the brunch, or perhaps a different family member offers to host the brunch, or you and your partner will host it.

A whole brunch may not be in the budget or of interest to you! If this is the case, and you still want to do something special for your guests the morning after your wedding, you can contact your hotel concierge and see if you can provide a light continental breakfast. An additional option would be to contact a local coffee shop or breakfast place and see if guests of your wedding could potentially receive a discount. You would be supporting a local business and your guests will feel extra valued—a win-win!

—» ask mariah «—
Your Other Events Questions

I do not want to have a bridal luncheon, but still want to ensure I am honoring and thanking my loved ones for being a part of my wedding party. What is the best way to go about this?

There are plenty of ways that you can honor and thank your loved ones if you choose not to have an official bridal luncheon. Perhaps it is not in your budget, or maybe you simply do not want to have to plan/host an additional event. The purpose and message behind the bridal luncheon is much more important than the logistics and details. You may consider catering breakfast while everyone is getting ready for the wedding and giving any gifts or thank-you notes at this time. Another alternative would be to meet briefly before the rehearsal dinner. Again, the most important part of this idea is that you are carving out time and space specially dedicated to thanking your loved ones for their commitment and friendship.

We do not plan on having a traditional rehearsal dinner. Can we have a welcome party the night before the wedding instead?

Absolutely! Some people choose to rehearse the logistics with their wedding party and immediate family, then have a welcome party afterward. You can combine both ideas to make it work for your wedding style and vision.

Do we need to send out formal invitations for these other events?

You certainly do not need to. You might consider adding the details to your wedding website, or perhaps adding a card in your invitation bundle detailing the information for any additional events you are holding. Welcome parties and morning-after brunches specifically are optional, and typically do not require an RSVP.

Thank-You
Notes &
Post-Wedding
Tasks

You did it! The wedding might be over, but your work isn't quite yet. Sending out handwritten thank-you notes is one of those traditions you will want to stick to. Your wedding guests will expect one and, after all, taking the time to write and send them is simply the right thing to do. In the past, the bride would be responsible for sending out thank-you cards, but today it should be a joint effort between each partner. You will most likely find yourself writing a lot of thank-you notes throughout your entire planning process because of the events that lead up to your wedding.

The secret to not getting overwhelmed by thank-you notes? Keep up with them for each event as they happen. Remember that spreadsheet that you already made for invitations and managing RSVPs? Add a column(s) next to each guest's name for shower and wedding gifts. This will be a simple way to keep yourself organized as you are getting ready to send out the notes.

✻ Creating Thank-You Notes ✻

I urge you to have fun with creating your thank-you notes. You can have these notes created by your invitation designer, and even use similar colors and designs that fit your wedding branding. You can also display your new monogram—should you choose to use one—or have your new last name or initial included somewhere. If your photographer is able to send previews quickly enough, you can have a thank-you-card set made with a photograph from your wedding. If you are looking for a quicker or more budget-friendly option, there are plenty of pre-designed thank-you cards out there for you to use. The most important thing here is not the look of the cards or money you spent on them, but rather the time you took to write personal messages in each and every card instead of a generic, printed message.

Thank-you notes should absolutely be handwritten and signed by both partners. You can divide the work and decide who writes them, but they should each be personally signed by both of you. In terms of thank-you-note stationery, you have quite a few options for what route to take.

While you are busy sending out thank-you cards, here are some other things you will want to spend time doing after the big day is over:

- Plan your honeymoon, if you haven't done so at this point already. This will be for couples who are not going on their honeymoon immediately after the wedding.

- Make sure any rentals are returned to their proper locations/companies in a timely manner.

- Begin looking into having your wedding gown or outfit preserved, if you want to.

- Choose photos for an album, to hang up in your home, and to gift to family, friends, or wedding party members.

- Enjoy your time as a newlywed and keep busy to avoid the post-wedding blues.

When writing your thank-you notes, you want to get as personal as possible. Simply thanking the person/couple for attending your wedding/shower, or for their gift, is not going to cut it! A well-written thank-you note will tell a story, evoke an emotion, and give sincere thanks. The following are examples you can use as guides.

For a wedding gift (from a couple who attended your wedding):

Dear X and X,

What a joy it was to have you both as a part of our most special night. We had the most incredible time dancing the night away with you. Thank you for being there, and for your generous gift of $500. We could not have imagined such a celebration without you there. We hope to see you really soon. All of our love,

(Enter couple's names here)

TIP ❯ *When it comes to thanking someone for monetary gifts it is typical to note the exact amount in the thank-you note for a more personal touch. This also confirms that you received the exact amount that they intended to gift you. Some people will recommend that you tell your guest what you will be using the money for. I do not think this is necessary as that is something private between you and your partner. The only exception to this would be if you had a honeymoon fund, you may note some of the activities you did or have planned on your honeymoon.*

For your florist (or any vendor!):

Dear X and X Florist Team,

We can truly say that our wedding would not have been complete without your beautiful work. We are still in awe of how the flowers complemented our venue and brought all of our colors together. You truly made our vision come to life.

Thank you for all of your hard work to make our space look and feel so special on such an important day. We can't wait to recommend you to everyone! With love,

(Enter couple's names here)

❧ People to Thank ❧

Here is a list of thank-you notes to consider writing and sending:

- Your bridal/wedding shower host(s)
- Bridal/wedding shower gifts
- Wedding gifts (this includes money)
- Your wedding party
- Anyone who played a major part in the planning process
- Anyone who financially contributed/hosted any part of the wedding
- Vendors (can include a tip if applicable)
- Officiant
- The person who watched your dog or kids for each event
- Your esthetician who saved the day the week leading up to your shower
- The salesperson who helped you pick out your dream wedding outfit

Do you get the idea here? There is no such thing as too many thank-you notes! They truly go such a long way and say so much about your character as a couple.

—» ask mariah «—

Your After the Wedding & Thank-You Notes Questions

What is the proper timing for thank-you notes, according to etiquette?

In general, thank-you notes should be sent within seven to ten days of receiving a gift, and within three to five days of receiving help, a favor, or to thank a host. Wedding-related activities always get extra cushion time due to the high volume of thank-you notes, and extensive planning going on around the writing of them. While there is no rule to follow, my recommendation is to aim (key word: aim) to send your thank-you notes within two weeks of your shower, and within six weeks of your wedding.

What should we do if someone sent us a gift early, perhaps immediately upon receiving our shower or wedding invitations? Should we send them a thank-you note right away?

In this case, it would probably be best to send them a thank-you note within two weeks of receiving the gift, this way, they can rest assured that it arrived safely. If a gift arrives close enough to your shower or wedding day, you can wait until you send out the rest of the thank-you notes.

When is it too late to send a thank-you note?

Never! There may be extenuating circumstances that force you to put off your thank-you-note writing. While you may have some guests looking for one, it's better to send a note late than to not send it at all. There is no need to point out or explain its tardiness when you send it, as that will take the focus away from the purpose of the note itself.

TIP ❯ *Writing and sending thank-you notes can certainly be a daunting task. Viewing it as a lovely tradition and gratitude practice will help ease you into the time-consuming activity. Set the scene for yourself so you can make the most out of your thank-you-note writing. Make your favorite drink, put on some comforting music, light a candle, and try your best to enjoy the process!*

We are a bilingual family; do we send out two different thank-you cards?

Since each thank-you note should be individually handwritten, you can customize each card depending on what language that particular guest speaks This is one of the many reasons I recommend personalized notes over the same printed, generic card for every guest.

How can we ensure our thank-you notes are accessible for a guest who is disabled?

Similar to how you handled your engagement announcements, save-the-dates, etc., you may have to make personal phone calls to thank any guests who would not be able to enjoy a thank-you card in the same way as other guests.

What happens if we receive a gift that was sent to our home and it arrives broken?

There is a good chance that you may put some breakable household items on your registry. With that being said, there is also the chance that the breakable items don't make it to your home in one piece. If you are able to handle this without involving the guest who sent it, that would be ideal! Most of your gifts will come with a gift receipt. Even if it does not, if you know where it came from, take it upon yourself to deal directly with the store's customer service. Chances are, they will be accommodating!

f you find yourself in a situation where you do not know where the gift was ourchased, and there is no gift receipt, it is absolutely acceptable to reach out to the person who sent the gift. Trust me, they would not want you to end up with a broken gift!

TIP > *If you return or exchange a gift for any reason, be sure to note what the original gift was so you are sending a thank-you note for the gift you received!*

A gift was mailed to our house before the wedding, but there was no card or return address. We have no idea who it is from. How do we handle this?

Your first step is to determine whether or not the gift came from your registry. You may be able to find out who sent it from there. Next, if it came from a specific store, you could call the store to try to track down who ourchased it. If you are unable to do these things, or they do not help solve the mystery, it may be time to glance back at that trusteed spreadsheet to work it out by process of elimination. This is obviously a tricky situation because you want to make sure guests are thanked properly for their gifts, out you also don't want to find yourself poking around to see who sent what. You also don't want to call anyone out for not giving a gift (even though they should have!).

f you went through all of these steps, and you are still completely stumped, you can send out a more generic thank-you card to any remaining guests for celebrating with you and thank them for their generosity. It will be a happy compromise for a sticky situation such as this one.

References

www.brides.com

www.theknot.com

Fox, Sue. *Wedding Etiquette for Dummies* (Wiley, 2010).

Post, Anna, et al. *Emily Post's Wedding Etiquette* (William Morrow, 2014).

Thank You

This book is a dream come true, and it truly "took a village," as they say. First and foremost, I want to thank the Quarto team for believing in me and giving me these blank pages to share my love for modern etiquette. I also want to thank my family: Ryan, Mom, Dad, Maddy, and Stevie for their unwavering support, and keeping me afloat on the days I couldn't imagine this "little business" was going to work. And last but certainly not least, I want to thank my OSE community and clients: You fuel my mission and this book would not be possible without you. I am truly grateful.

About the Author

As a certified etiquette trainer and founder of Old Soul Etiquette, Mariah Grumet's mission is to bring an intentional sparkle back to a lost art. Her method of teaching puts a modern and approachable twist on timeless lessons of etiquette, manners, and respect, to help her clients and community create stronger connections, distinguish themselves, and reach their full potential in their personal and professional lives. Mariah works with individuals of all ages and backgrounds located across the globe. Old Soul Etiquette's services include private consulting, group sessions, webinars, speaking engagements, and special events on the following topics: youth, social, dining, and business etiquette; personal branding; wedding preparation; style consulting; and more.

Mariah is a graduate of the University of Delaware with a bachelor's degree in fashion merchandising. She has been certified to teach etiquette through The Protocol School of Palm Beach, is a graduate of The English Manner and Beaumont Etiquette's Train the Trainer Grade One Program with Merit, and is a member of the International Etiquette Trainer Society. Mariah has been seen in *Forbes, Fox News, Southern Living, The New York Post, TODAY, Travel and Leisure, Brides,* and more.

10 9 8 7 6 5 4 3 2

ISBN: 978-1-63106-972-7

Digital edition published in 2024
eISBN: 978-0-7603-8501-2

Library of Congress Control Number: 2023940396

Publisher: Rage Kindelsperger
Editorial Director: Erin Canning
Creative Director: Laura Drew
Senior Art Director: Marisa Kwek
Managing Editor: Cara Donaldson
Editor: Keyla Pizarro-Hernández
Cover Design and Book Layout: Angela Williams
Author Headshot on Page 6: Maddie Sullivan Photography

Printed in China